estherpress

Books for Courageous Women

ESTHER PRESS VISION

Publishing diverse voices that encourage and equip women to walk courageously in the light of God's truth for such a time as this.

BIBLICAL STATEMENT OF PURPOSE

"For if you keep silent at this time, relief and deliverance will rise for the Jews from another place, but you and your father's house will perish. And who knows whether you have not come to the kingdom for such a time as this?"

Esther 4:14 (ESV)

A Table in the Wilderness

A STUDY ON GOD'S GOODNESS

AN INTERACTIVE
BIBLE STUDY

Includes Six-Session
Video Series

LINA
ABUJAMRA

A Table in the Wilderness

A STUDY ON GOD'S GOODNESS

📍 MAPPING THE FOOTSTEPS OF GOD SERIES

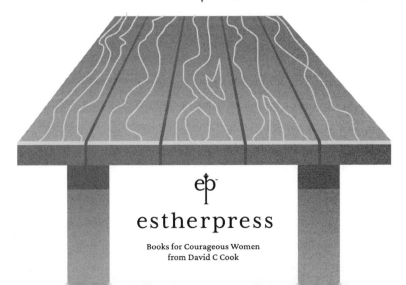

eþ

estherpress

Books for Courageous Women
from David C Cook

A TABLE IN THE WILDERNESS
Published by Esther Press
an imprint of David C Cook
4050 Lee Vance Drive
Colorado Springs, CO 80918 U.S.A.

Integrity Music Limited, a Division of David C Cook
Brighton, East Sussex BN1 2RE, England

Esther Press, David C Cook, and related logos are trademarks of David C Cook.

ISBN 978-0-8307-8423-3
eISBN 978-0-8307-8424-0

The Team: Susan McPherson, Jeff Gerke, James Hershberger, Jack Campbell, Susan Murdock
Cover Design: Emily Weigel
Author Cover Bio Photo: Jake Preedin

Printed in the United States of America
First Edition 2024

1 2 3 4 5 6 7 8 9 10

103023

To Sam, who has never missed a feast or the planning of one.

Contents

Meet the Author

Lina AbuJamra is a pediatric ER doctor now practicing telemedicine and the founder of Living with Power Ministries. Her vision is to bring hope to the world by connecting biblical answers to everyday life. A popular Bible teacher, podcaster, and conference speaker, Lina is the author of *Through the Desert*, her first Bible study in the Mapping the Footsteps of God series by David C Cook. Her other recent books include *Don't Tell Anyone You're Reading This* by Forefront Books and *Fractured Faith* by Moody Publishers.

Lina ministers to singles through her Moody Radio show, *Today's Single Christian*, and provides medical care and humanitarian aid in disaster areas and to refugees in Lebanon and Ukraine. Learn more about her at livingwithpower.org.

Acknowledgments

I am mostly grateful for my assistant, Irina, who always has my back and is a gift of God's goodness to me. This project wouldn't have been complete without her! I remain grateful to my agent, Don Pape, who continues to offer his support and vision for Christ's kingdom here on earth. To Diana, my sister, I love you much more than I take time to tell you. Thank you and your family for opening your dinner table for me daily.

I'm grateful to every man and woman who has listened to me teach. Our Thursday-night Facebook Live community has been a place of love and support. Thank you for continuing to show up.

For the team at David C Cook—thank you for believing in me and giving me a chance to dance for Jesus. Teaching the Bible is the heartbeat of my soul. Thanks to Susan McPherson, Jeff Gerke, and the entire marketing team for creating something out of my words.

I would like to acknowledge you too, dear reader, for making time for this study in an age of distractions and a plethora of Bible studies. Your commitment to God's Word moves me.

And to Jesus, the bread of life—nothing is impossible with You. You alone are the reason I'm here.

Introduction

I recently had a life-altering realization: I need Bible study in my life.

I don't do Bible study as an optional activity or simply because I have extra time on my hands. As a busy practicing physician who also runs a global ministry, I don't have a lot of margin. I don't do Bible study because I love the way each study is divided into five days of homework and weekly teaching lessons. In fact, the repetitive monotony of a typical study sometimes drives me crazy. And I don't do Bible study because I follow some Christian authors and can't wait to devour the next thing they release. Even if I were a rabid fan of some Christian authors, I am way too cool to admit it.

No. I literally *need* Bible study in order to make it through my Christian life. While I love my own daily time with God, the discipline of studying the Bible with other people in a systematic fashion is essential to my spiritual formation. Honestly, without Bible study, I'd have drifted from the faith by now.

I grew up in the Sunday school era and gave my life to Jesus as a child. In those days, people gathered regularly to study the Bible—sometimes several times a week. The Sunday school system eventually morphed into the small groups movement. Small groups stalled because of COVID-19 and the much more dangerous pandemic of human apathy. It has become evident to me that skipping Bible study is natural for most of us who call ourselves Christians. It can also be quite deadly.

If you want the life squeezed out of your Christian walk, stop studying the Bible. If you want to sink in a world gone mad, de-prioritize the time you spend digging deep into God's Word. If you want to become stale and burned out, stop asking God why He gave us His precious Word and how He intends to use it to nourish our daily lives.

But if you want to thrive, if you want to be transformed, and if you want to feel like you're alive again, then join me on this journey in Bible study.

If you want the life squeezed out of your Christian walk, stop studying the Bible.

I promise that on some days during this study, you will need to fight for the time to get through the homework. I promise you that some days will seem boring. You will be tempted to cut corners, and sometimes you will. You will be forced to skip some days, and that's okay. But keep on showing up. Day after day, week after week, force yourself to immerse in God's Word. Sink into the pages of Scripture and yield yourself to the Holy Spirit, and you will find the abundant life Jesus promised.

Look around you, my friend. If we've ever needed to be refreshed, now is the time. We need God's Word to wash *into* our souls. We need God's Spirit to renew us from the filth of the broken culture we're living in. We need each other too. We need to hold each other to a higher standard. We need to be pressed and prodded to become more than we've settled for. We need fresh eyes to see all that we've hoped to become. We need the Lord like never before, and the place to find Him is in His Word.

If this is your first Bible study with me, let me warn you that I can be intense—but I think I'm mellowing with age. I'm an ER doctor by training and practice, and some would say by personality. Don't let my intensity scare you. You'll get used to me in no time. I'm thrilled you've stepped out in faith and signed up for this journey. We're going to have a blast together.

If you've been with me before, perhaps in one of the other studies in the Mapping the Footsteps of God series, I'm so honored you're back. Didn't you love making your way through the desert with God?

We're in for a treat during the next six weeks. We're going to feast on God's *goodness*. If you like food, you will love this study. If food isn't really your thing, don't worry; this study isn't about food at all. It's about God's goodness to us in unexpected places.

I'm guessing you're in need of some goodness in your life. So am I! I am a recovering Eeyore, but the more I taste and see of God's goodness, the harder it becomes to hang on to my crusty outlook. Instead, I've found myself delighted to be invited to God's table in the wilderness, where His goodness overflows.

What do you know—you've been invited too, and I'm so glad you said yes! I'm thrilled you're joining me on this journey through God's Word as we feast together on the goodness of our God!

Lina

About This Study

This study is about God's goodness.

What does it mean that God is good? *Merriam-Webster's Dictionary* describes *goodness* as "the quality or state of being good."[1] Easton's *Illustrated Bible Dictionary* says that God's goodness is "a perfection of his character which he exercises toward his creatures according to their various circumstances and relations."[2]

In other words, God's goodness is His benevolence toward you and me. God is good because He loves us and wants what's best for us. One of the most important lessons I'm learning and hope to teach you in our time together is that what God knows is best for us isn't always what we think is best for us. That's where many of us get stuck in the Christian life.

But think about this: one of the most amazing ways God revealed His goodness to us is through food. Who knew, right? It might sound hard to believe, yet from the very first pages of Genesis, we learn that God created food for humans to enjoy and to be filled with. Throughout Scripture, we continue to see God setting up a table so His people may be filled.

I don't know about you, but I think it's fascinating that only humans eat at a table. While that might seem obvious, I find it riveting. I believe it's intentional and symbolic of the deeper meaning of food. The table is where people gather to do more than just eat. We laugh together at the table. Sometimes we cry, and other times we sit silently, reassuring each other that our present problems are not the end of our story. And yes, through it all, we eat together too. The table is a place to connect. It's the place many of us feel most alive.

It's no wonder, then, that God has a way of showing up at tables. In both the Old Testament and the New Testament, stories of God at tables are woven into the narrative of Scripture. In fact, some of the most critical aspects of the spiritual life take place at tables: Passover and Communion.

Here's what N. T. Wright has written about tables: "When Jesus himself wanted to explain to his disciples what his forthcoming death was all about, he didn't give them a theory, he gave them a meal."[3]

Sharing a table nourishes us both physically and spiritually. When you think about it, food must be one of God's love languages. That He created us to experience the delight of taste is an expression of His love. If the fact that He regularly invites His people to the table to lavish them with delight isn't a sign of His goodness, then I'm not sure what is!

We're going to study five of the tables God invites us to throughout His Word. We'll see how unexpected each one is and how often that table is set up in the least likely place—the wilderness. In the most unexpected places, God revels in delighting His children with His goodness.

Everything God does has a purpose. Every detail in Scripture points us toward a greater understanding of who He is—His character and His ways. Every part of every meal has a reason. And while God cares about our physical hunger, He cares even more about filling our spiritual hunger.

Here's what our time together is going to look like:

- The introductory week, including session 1's video and follow-up discussion, will provide a framework for why God chooses to feed us when He wants to teach us about His goodness.
- Week 1: The Passover, or the table of salvation, is the table God uses to deliver His people from slavery.
- Week 2: The table of unexpected belonging is the story of Mephibosheth being invited to King David's table. This table is where we will feast on God's goodness to us in the places we expect it the least.
- Week 3: The table of overflowing satisfaction takes place at the wedding in Cana. Jesus shows us how abundant and extravagant His goodness truly is.

- Week 4: The table of remembrance is the celebration of the Lord's Supper. We will feast on God's goodness in the seasons and places we're so apt to forget it.
- Week 5: The last table is the feast of eternal celebration, the marriage supper of the Lamb, where we will learn God's plan to feed us with His goodness eternally.

Our focus will be on God's goodness to us in the most unexpected places. Though we'll be mapping the footsteps of God across the entire Scriptures, and though we will cover a lot of ground and look at a number of people and places, the hero in this Bible study is God! He is the one our hearts long for. He is the one we seek to know. While our time in Scripture will lead us to know ourselves better, our ultimate goal in Bible study is to know God more. The more we know God, the more we can trust Him. The more we trust God, the more we will experience joy in our wilderness places.

If you've ever found yourself hungry for joy, this study is for you. If you feel stuck in your life, burned out, or weighed down by life's duties, this study is for you. Even if you're in a good place right now, *A Table in the Wilderness* will delight you as we review the abundant goodness of God to His children. My prayer is that God will reveal Himself clearly to you through this study and that you begin to sense His presence deeply as you dig into the reality of who He is as revealed through His Word.

How It Will Look

A Table in the Wilderness is a six-week Bible study. It is my hope that you'll be doing this study with a group, either in person or online, because you'll get the most benefit from sharing your answers with others in discussion. But if you're doing this as an individual study, the same session structure will apply.

Each session begins with a brief overview of what we'll be studying for the week. Then, during your group's meeting time, you'll watch a video of me teaching the basis for the lesson. Fill in the blanks in this book by watching the video and discuss it together using the Video Group Discussion Questions. If you're on your own, answer the questions in this book and meditate on them prayerfully.

You can structure your group's meeting time however you'd like, but here's a sample flow to the meetings to get you started:

- Snacks and fellowship as you gather
- Greeting and introduction
- Opening prayer
- Recap discussion of the previous week's homework
- Watch the video (fill in the blanks as you watch)
- Video group discussion (either discuss as a group or complete on your own)
- Prayer requests (for individual study, you may want to start a prayer journal)
- Closing prayer and dismissal

When you go home, you'll work on your daily interactive material on your own. Each week has five days' worth of material so you can dig deeply into God's goodness to His people in unexpected places. At the end of each week, you'll find a section called "Praying through Scripture," where you'll place yourself in the sandals of the people of the Bible and really soak in the passages we're studying.

At the end of this book, I've placed some helpful resources:

- a QR code as a quick link to all the videos
- a leader's guide with tips for guiding a group through this study
- spiritual exercises (*lectio divina*) for each session
- a self-reflection tool
- the answers to the fill-in-the-blank questions from the videos
- the endnotes

Note: The final session won't have any homework or spiritual exercises. You'll gather to watch the video, discuss it, and then maybe you'll want to celebrate a meal together at a table of your own!

If you've ever wondered whether God's goodness has bypassed you, this study is for you. Perhaps you're stuck in a wilderness right now. My hope is that you will find abundant joy at the table God has spread for you, even in your present wilderness.

Ready to do this? Let's jump right in. Or as they say at the table, *bon appetit!*

Session 1: Introduction

Why a Table in the Wilderness?

Psalm 23

Watch the session 1 video now. The video is available at DavidCCook.org/access, with access code TABLE.

1. A table in the wilderness is a daily reminder that God created us with the need to be

_____.

2. A table in the wilderness is God's _____ for our most basic needs in our most difficult places.

3. A table in the wilderness is a picture of God's _____ to us in our most unexpected places.

4. A table in the wilderness is a resting stop for _____ and _____ as we make our way home.

Video Group Discussion Questions

After watching the video, discuss the following questions in your group.

♀ What comes to your mind when you think about a table in the wilderness?

♀ Why did you sign up for this Bible study? What do you hope to get out of it?

♀ In Psalm 23:5, David wrote, "You prepare a table before me in the presence of my enemies; you anoint my head with oil; my cup overflows." Think about the places in your life where you long for God's overflowing blessing in the presence of your enemies. Share one of these difficult places with your group.

♀ God created food to remind us of our need to be filled. Spiritually speaking, what are you most hungry for in your Christian life?

📍 If you could have a meal with any two to four people in the world, who would you choose, and why?

Goodness

good·ness | ˈgu̇d-nəs
Definition of *God's goodness*

Goodness of God

a perfection of his character which he exercises toward his creatures according to their various circumstances and relations (Ps. 145:8, 9; 103:8; 1 John 4:8). Viewed generally, it is benevolence; as exercised with respect to the miseries of his creatures it is mercy, pity, compassion, and in the case of impenitent sinners, long-suffering patience; as exercised in communicating favour on the unworthy it is grace. "Goodness and justice are the several aspects of one unchangeable, infinitely wise, and sovereign moral perfection. God is not sometimes merciful and sometimes just, but he is eternally infinitely just and merciful." God is infinitely and unchangeably good (Zeph. 3:17), and his goodness is incomprehensible by the finite mind (Rom. 11:35, 36). "God's goodness appears in two things, giving and forgiving."[4]

Most often God's goodness is His faithfulness shown in the covenant: redemption from Egypt and care in the wilderness (Ex. 18:9); the gift of the land (Josh. 24:20); teaching and law (Jer. 6:16); the temple (Ezra 3:11); forgiveness (Hos. 3:5); care for the needy (Ps. 68:10); strength in time of trouble (Hab. 1:7); and the promise of restoration and a new covenant (Zech. 8:15), now fulfilled gloriously in Jesus Christ (Titus 3:4).[5]

Week 1: The Table of Salvation— When I Need to Be Rescued

Psalm 34:8

"Oh, taste and see that the LORD is good! Blessed is the man who takes refuge in him!"

Introduction

I was invited to speak to a group of singles in Colorado in the middle of ski season some time ago. I was looking forward to the event and had finally made my way to the lodge when I decided to make a quick run to the store for some necessities. Being from Green Bay, Wisconsin, I considered myself an expert at driving in the snow and didn't think twice about the winter weather when I took off in the rented vehicle.

I was about a mile away from the lodge when the most unexpected thing happened to me: I got stuck in a snowbank. I tried to get myself out of my mess but couldn't. The harder I tried, the more stuck I got. I looked for my phone to call for help when I, again unexpectedly, noticed that I had not brought my phone with me on this quick trip to the store. I was in trouble. The event would be starting in a couple of hours, and all I had was the hope that someone might come driving by and help me out.

The longer I waited, the more it dawned on me that I was on a fairly remote road without much traffic. I thought about walking back to the lodge, but the very idea was daunting. I was too far away from the lodge to walk, and it was too cold outside to risk it anyway.

So I prayed. I cried out to God with increasing desperation. What other options did I have out there in the snowy wilderness? I pictured every worst-case scenario. I hoped that eventually the folks at the conference might notice my absence from the evening session and send out a search party for me. I prayed I wouldn't freeze before they showed up.

I'll spare you the drama and tell you that, eventually, someone did show up. Luckily, that person had a phone, and it was only a matter of time before I moved past the fear of dying to the embarrassment of having gotten stuck in the snowbank in the first place. Needless to say, I had a good story to tell that night at my speaking event.

The thing about life is that most of us don't realize we're stuck until it's too late to notice that we have no way out of the mess. Whether it's a snowbank or a relationship, most of us don't plan on getting stuck. We start out excited and hopeful. We look forward to the adventure ahead. We barely think about the fact that we might need help until we realize that we do.

Yet almost every situation in life is an invitation for us to cry out for help. We are living in the wilderness, but we notice that fact only when disaster strikes. And when it does, we figure we can get ourselves out of our own messes—until we can't!

The thing about life is that most of us don't realize we're stuck until it's too late to notice that we have no way out of the mess.

It's when we run out of options that we finally cry out for help. It's when the waiting goes on and the rescue is delayed that our cries become more desperate and serious. These are the cries that move the heart of God.

These are the places where God invites us to the first of His tables we're going to look at: the table of salvation.

God loves to save His people. The harder our situation becomes, the more His goodness abounds. The more desperate our cry, the more His heart is moved toward us in mercy. I love that about God. We serve a God who doesn't take joy in our pain but sits with us in our pain … and then redeems it for His purposes and our good. We serve a God who not only *can* save us but wants to.

This week, we'll spend time at the table of salvation. Here, we will get to know this God who invites His people to be rescued. It's one of the most important tables in the Old Testament—the Passover table. This table has been commemorated by the Jewish people every year from the Old Testament period right on through to today. The story behind the Passover table is one of a people who needed rescuing but didn't cry for help until they were extremely desperate.

Perhaps you're in a desperate place right now. You're stuck in the wilderness season of your life, except yours feels more like a Chicago winter—never ending! You feel like you have no hope of rescue. Perhaps like me, you've metaphorically misplaced your phone. The only thing left to do is pray.

If that's you, you're in the perfect place to witness God's goodness. His goodness shines best in our most unexpected places. God's invitation is for us to sit at His table of salvation. His promise is rescue. My prayer for you this week is that you will let God's Word lead you where His Spirit longs to take you. Receive all He has for you as you seek His freedom and joy.

Like the people of Israel received, this week is your invitation to sit at God's table and feast on His goodness in the places where you need to be rescued.

Day 1: The People's Plight

Reading: Exodus 1 and 2:23–25

Theme: God always hears our cries for help and saves us.

I've spent the bulk of my medical practice in emergency care, and if I've learned one thing in that line of work, it's that you can't dream about fixing a problem until you know what the problem is.

The Bible is the story of God saving His people from death and hell. From the beginning of Genesis until the last pages of Revelation, the entire story is one of redemption. Adam and Eve sinned in the garden of Eden in what is referred to as the fall of mankind. They needed a Savior. That's when God initiated the story of redemption.

The Bible tells the story of God's love and His plan to get His people out of trouble. Though the Bible spans thousands of years and tells of many individuals, the overarching storyline remains the same: redemption—God restoring His people to Himself.

In the Old Testament, the redemption thread is woven through the chosen people of God: Israel. That part of the story started when God called Abraham to follow Him. By the time we get to Exodus 1, Abraham's family has grown quite a bit—and boy, do they need to be rescued! This week's homework will focus on the plight of the people of Israel at a time when they were stuck in a place they needed to be delivered from.

Despite God's promise to give Abraham's descendants a land of their own, Egypt didn't feel anything like the Promised Land the people of Israel had dreamed of. When we meet them in Exodus 1, the people of Israel were at their wits' end. It will become evident as we study our passage today that the more desperate the people felt, the more glory would be given to God when He would rescue them. Let's fill in the details by focusing on our text for today.

♦ Read Exodus 1 and summarize what sort of trouble the people of Israel were facing.

⦿ Why did the king of Egypt hate the people of Israel?

The people of Israel were hated because they were thriving. They didn't deserve to be punished for being successful, but the cultural context they were living in made them a threat to the Egyptians. The result was disastrous for them.

⦿ Read Exodus 1:15–16. How bad did things get for the people of Israel?

⦿ Have you ever been treated unfairly because of your background or race? How did that impact you and make you feel?

The pushback the people of Israel faced in that time was substantial, but it wasn't surprising. In fact, God had predicted that this would happen hundreds of years before it did.

⦿ Read Genesis 15:12–16. What did God prophetically tell Abraham about his descendants?

♥ Does it bother you to know that God knew ahead of time that the people of Israel would be mistreated? Why, or why not?

♥ Why do you think God didn't save His people from pain when He could have done so?

God is never unaware of the pain we're enduring. He not only knows about it but in His sovereignty, He allows it. He has a purpose for every painful thing we experience. The challenge for us is that we don't clearly understand why. The people of Israel certainly didn't. They were hurting. They eventually hurt so badly that they cried out for help.

♥ Read Exodus 2:23–25. Describe the emotions the people of Israel were feeling.

♥ Who did the people of Israel cry out for help to?

Whether the people of Israel were crying out to God or not is hard to know, but what God's Word tells us *for sure* is that God heard their cry for help. God *heard*. God *saw*. God *knew* their pain. And God had a plan to rescue them.

📍 Read Exodus 3:6–10. Write down the ways God described Himself in verse 6. Why was that relevant here?

📍 Simply put, what was God's plan for His people?

For four hundred years, the people of God suffered in Egypt. Their pain became progressively more unbearable. It took the people four hundred years to finally cry out to God in desperation. Four hundred years is a long time. Most of us get tired of waiting after forty minutes, let alone four hundred years!

📍 Do you ever wonder why God takes His time in answering us? Why do you think He does?

◉ Are you in a place of waiting right now? How does knowing that God heard the people of Israel give you the hope to go on?

The Christian life is a life of waiting ... because waiting is about trust. The more we wait on God for rescue, the more our trust in Him is stretched and the stronger our faith becomes. While we might think that God has forgotten about us in the waiting, the truth is that God is just getting started with us when we reach our point of desperation. God's goodness is best seen when our pain is most palpable.

God's goodness is best seen when our pain is most palpable.

Our focus today has been on the people's plight. Life had gotten hard for the people of Israel, and they needed rescuing. The good news was that rescue was on the way. In the remainder of this week, we're going to study exactly how God planned to rescue His people. He ended up doing it in the most unexpected way, through a table in the wilderness.

Let's Make This Personal

◉ Where in your life right now do you need to be rescued? What situation are you facing that you can't get yourself out of? Where has the waiting lingered? Write down your heart's cry to God as you face the unknown.

Today's Take Home Point

Just because God hasn't acted on your behalf yet doesn't mean He is unaware of your pain.

Final Thought

 As you feel the weight of your current suffering, what might God be inviting you to in your present painful places?

Celebrate Good

 As you consider our time in God's Word, write down one good thing you can celebrate in your life today.

Day 2: God's Perfect Plan

Reading: Exodus 12:1–13

Theme: While we need physical food to survive, it's spiritual food that gives us life.

Are you wondering when we're going to start talking about food? And tables? And feasts? Don't worry; it's coming—and it may take you by surprise. I mean, the last thing we might expect in a showdown between Pharaoh and Moses is a meal! Yet God's goodness often takes us by surprise in the most unexpected places.

As Christians, we're told that God is good all the time, and we believe it up to a point. Yet I've caught myself again and again utterly surprised when God reveals His goodness *to me*. It's not that I don't believe that God is good, but I often struggle to believe that He is good to me!

I suppose part of the problem is that we frequently link God's goodness to the outcomes we want. We pray with bated breath hoping that God won't hold back, that He won't change His mind, that He'll actually answer us. We're delighted by His goodness when He gives us what we want. But one of the things I'm learning is that God's goodness is far better than the things He provides for us. God's goodness is Himself. God's goodness is His presence. God's goodness is ours whether He gives us what we ask for or not.

Today's homework will begin a deeper study of one of the most important tables God set before His people in the Old Testament. It's a table that becomes a ritual for the people of Israel and a picture not only of all God had promised their father, Abraham, but also of all that was still to be fulfilled in the Messiah. Today, we'll spend our time reflecting on the Passover table, the table of salvation.

📍 Read Exodus 12:1–13. Jot down some of your impressions as you read the passage. What verse sticks out to you the most? Copy it here.

⦿ Of all the ways God could have led the people of Israel out of Egypt, why do you think He chose a meal to do so?

It's fascinating when you think about it. The people of Israel had spent four hundred years in Egypt, mostly as slaves. By the time we pick up their story in Exodus 1, they wanted out. They were desperate for a savior—any savior.

In Exodus 3, God finally called a deliverer, Moses, to lead the people out of Egypt, fully aware that there would be massive resistance from the king of Egypt, Pharaoh. The pages of Scripture that lead up to Exodus 12 are a description of nine plagues with which God revealed His power both to His people and to the Egyptians. The plagues were meant to encourage the people of Israel that their God was strong enough to save them *and* to glorify God in the eyes of the people of Egypt.

Despite God revealing His power, the people of Egypt were slow to understand the extent of who God is. Frankly, even the people of Israel had a hard time fully comprehending the awesome power of God. Though they saw His great works, they still feared that they would remain stuck in Egypt forever.

Think about it: God sent nine plagues that should have been enough to convince Pharaoh to let the people of Israel go and to embolden the people of Israel to rest in their God. First came the turning of water into blood, then the frogs, the lice, the flies, the pestilence on the livestock, the boils, the hail, the locusts, and the darkness that settled on the face of the earth. And still Pharaoh stubbornly refused to let the people go, and still the people of Israel struggled with doubt.

The plagues were not an afterthought. God wasn't surprised at Pharaoh's resistance. In fact, God had predicted it. All along, God was setting up the final plague, the one that led to the first Passover meal, which would become symbolic of God's saving power of His people. We're going to focus on the Passover table in this week's homework.

I mentioned in the introduction that food is God's love language. From the very first pages of the Scriptures, we see the gift of food that God gives His people. In Genesis 1–2, right after God created humans, He fed them.

♀ Read Genesis 2:8–9, 15–17. What did God instruct Adam and Eve to do with the food He had created for them?

♀ Were there any boundaries that God gave His people regarding food?

♀ Why do you think God created man with the need to eat?

While it's impossible to live without food, God could have easily created human beings who did not need to eat to survive. But He didn't. He created man and woman as creatures who needed to eat in order to make it, to live, to thrive.

♀ What spiritual implications can be drawn from God's plan to feed His people?

As important as food is to the human body, it seems as if the message God is sending us is bigger than just about a meal. Perhaps God is reminding us that more than the food that we eat to nourish our bodies, it's spiritual nourishment that we need to really thrive.

 Read Deuteronomy 8:3. I love this verse. Take some time to rewrite the verse here and start memorizing it. The more you hide God's Word in your heart, the more God will use it to encourage you when you need it.

> More than the food we eat to nourish our bodies, it's spiritual nourishment that we need to really thrive.

We need more than mere food to survive. We need the Word of God to make it through life. Throughout Scripture, we see a pattern in which God used physical food as a picture with spiritual implications. What we eat matters. What we eat transforms us. What we eat and how we eat it make all the difference in the world. Let's look at how God used food to symbolize deeper spiritual lessons.

 Read Exodus 12:1–13 again. List the various elements of the meal that God instructed the people of Israel to prepare for the first Passover.

Here is a table to help you understand the elements of the first Passover and their meaning.[6]

Element	Significance
A lamb without blemish prepared for households and eaten together (vv. 3-5).	The Messiah was to be one body, broken for all, eaten by all, to help believers keep aware of their unity as members of one body.
The blood put on two doorposts and the lintel of the houses in which it was eaten (v. 7).	The blood was a sign to Israel and to God that no harm would come to the household during the night of destruction of the firstborn of Egypt. Christ's blood was shed to atone for our sins and set us apart as a nation holy to God.
The people were to eat the flesh that night, roasted on the fire (v. 8) ...	The Passover meal was to be eaten with a readiness to leave Egypt immediately. Roasting over fire was the fastest and simplest way to cook meat. The whole meal was about faith: it was the people's faith in God's promises that made them ready for a sudden departure. They were ready to move at a moment's notice—by faith.
... with unleavened bread (v. 8) ...	Bread made without yeast was designated to minimize the time of preparation. Later, God instructed the Israelites to celebrate the Feast of Unleavened Bread right after the Passover. They were commanded to purge their homes of leaven (Ex. 12:14-20), symbolizing separation from Egypt, freedom from bondage and sin, and a reminder that they were the new people of God. In the New Testament, leaven symbolized contamination with the world and something to avoid (1 Cor. 5:8; Luke 12:1).

... and bitter herbs they shall eat it (v. 8).	The bitter herbs were a reminder of the bitter experience of slavery in Egypt, from which God was about to deliver them (Ex. 1:14).
And you shall let none of it remain until the morning; anything that remains until the morning you shall burn (v. 10).	That any remaining meat had to be consumed by fire in the morning pointed to the sacred sense of the meal and to the fact that the people had to trust that God would provide for them the next day. The Passover was more a meal of religious observance than a meal to provide sustenance over time.
In this manner you shall eat it: with your belt fastened, your sandals on your feet, and your staff in your hand. And you shall eat it in haste (v. 11).	By eating the Passover meal dressed for the journey, the Israelites demonstrated their trust in God and their belief that He was able to deliver them from the power of Pharaoh.

Tomorrow's time will focus more on the lamb portion of the meal, but for today, let's start to build on the meaning of the first table, the Passover table, that God was preparing for His children.

○ Read Exodus 12:12–13 again. What did God promise would happen to those whose doors were not covered by the blood of the lamb?

○ Does God's plan to kill all the firstborns of Egypt seem harsh to you, or does it seem justified?

◉ Read Exodus 1:15–16. What kind of man was Pharaoh, based on what you read in these verses? Does Pharaoh's cruelty change the way you view God's judgment on the people of Egypt?

It's fascinating, isn't it, how quickly we form judgments on the things we conclude are right and wrong. We act as if we know what's best. We forget that we are not God. *God* is God. We forget that the goodness of God is often expressed by mercy in the places where judgment is deserved. Scripture is written not for us to judge God but to understand Him better, to know Him more deeply, and to choose Him even when His plans don't make sense to us.

◉ Who do you identify with more as you read the story of the first Passover meal: the people of Israel or the people of Egypt?

If I had to guess, I would think that most of us read the story of the first Passover and identify with the people of Israel. We suspect that we deserve to be saved. We see ourselves in those people struggling and praying and waiting for the Savior's deliverance. But what if the alternative were true? What if in the story of the first Passover, you and I saw ourselves not as who we want to be, but who we really are?

If God is good, what possible good could flow out of the death that took place on the night of the first Passover?

This first Passover table was not a leisurely meal to be savored and enjoyed. It was a meal eaten in haste. In a most unusual way, God's perfect plan to save His people happened over a meal through a table in the wilderness. What an unexpected turn of events. We will spend even more time reflecting on the elements of the Passover meal tomorrow, but for today, let's rejoice that our God is not only mighty to save but eager to do it!

Let's Make This Personal

📍 Have you ever been tempted to judge God's actions by what you think is right? Where in your life might you be judging God right now? Won't you take some time and ask Him to forgive you for it?

Today's Take Home Point

Even when we misunderstand His ways,
God's plans are for our good.

Final Thought

📍 As you meditate on God's plan to rescue His people, where in your life is God inviting you to come out of slavery?

Celebrate Good

📍 As you consider our time in God's Word, write down one good thing you've learned about God that you can celebrate in your life today.

Day 3: About the Lamb

Reading: Exodus 12:1–13, 21–22

Theme: The Passover table isn't about the food—it's about the Lamb.

Every holiday has its special food. When I think about Thanksgiving, it's all about the turkey. And when I think about Christmas, it's the eggnog or cranberry sauce that takes center stage. At Easter, it's Easter eggs, and on July Fourth, it's grilled bratwurst. Birthdays are all about cake. It seems like every holiday has its symbolic food. Food has meaning, and a table becomes the place where we celebrate that meaning.

When it comes to the Passover table, it's the lamb that gets the spotlight. God's plan to save His people came down to a lamb. But not just any lamb prepared any old way. Much of what we read in Exodus 12 and other portions of the Old Testament (such as Lev. 22:20–21) focuses on the lamb and the way it was to be prepared. In our time together today, we're going to explore God's purpose for the lamb that was eaten as part of His plan to deliver the people of Israel from their slavery.

Read Exodus 12:3–13. Write down every detail you notice about the lamb.

The picture of the lamb as a sacrifice for sin is central to the Old Testament. Let's explore some of the history of the animal sacrifice leading up to the Passover table. For each passage of Scripture, write down the purpose of the sacrificial animal:

Genesis 4:1–7

Genesis 15:9–17

Genesis 22:13

By the time of Exodus 12, the idea that an animal was offered as a burnt offering was not new to the people of Israel. But the instructions God gave the people of Israel for the first Passover meal were very specific and meant to be followed precisely. Every detail had meaning. Write down what you think each of these elements of the offering meant:

Lamb without blemish:

One year old:

Killed at twilight:

The flesh of the lamb roasted:

None of the lamb should remain:

Lamb must be eaten in haste:

The blood must be on the doorposts:

It's impossible to fully appreciate the imagery of Passover without understanding that the lamb sacrificed to save the people of Israel was a glorious picture of Christ. Read each

of the following verses and jot down how Christ fulfills the picture of the lamb given in
Exodus 12.

John 1:29

1 Corinthians 5:7–8

Hebrews 9:12–14

Hebrews 9:22

1 Peter 1:17–19

Revelation 5:6

Think about the impossible scene that played out on the night of the Passover. Numbers
1:46 says that the Israelite army numbered well over 600,000 men. That puts the total number
of the Israelite population at an estimated two million people, which is a staggering figure to
imagine.

Divide that number into households and try to wrap your mind around the number of
lambs slain that night. One commentary, in reflecting on the magnitude of that night, reports
that the largest and most efficient cattle-processing plant in the United States has the ability
to process eight thousand cattle a day, but that would require twenty-two hundred employees
working around the clock. Almost eighty thousand farmers and ranchers are needed to care
for the six million sheep throughout the nation.

The commentary concludes: "What the people of Israel did was unfathomable—to have that many animals let alone butcher them all. All those sacrifices placed the people in a position to trust that God would rescue them, continue to feed them, continue to be their provider."[7]

Wow. Can you imagine that night? Can you imagine the faith it took to obey God's instructions? Perhaps it was because the people of Israel had seen God's power in the nine previous plagues that they were ready to obey God, or perhaps the pain of staying in Egypt was finally greater to them than the unknowns involved in leaving.

Can you imagine the faith it took to obey God's instructions?

But one thing we know for sure: it was only those who followed God's command and put the blood on their doorposts who were spared the judgment that the people of Egypt felt on that night.

♀ How does knowing the price it took to be rescued from slavery change your perception of the Passover?

It's all been about the lamb, that perfect lamb of God. Though the price was terribly high for the people of Israel to be rescued, that pales in comparison to what it cost Jesus to hang on the cross at Calvary. No table in the Old Testament points more clearly to the eventual sacrifice of Christ for our sin than the Passover table does.

If you've been thinking that the Passover table is about a meal, I hope today's time in Scripture has opened your eyes to the deeper significance of this precious lamb of God. This most vulnerable of all animals became the one whose blood was shed to save those who believed God enough to hide beneath its covering. In the end, it was the people's faith and obedience to God to put the blood on the doorposts that saved the children of Israel.

♦ As you consider the precious blood shed to rescue people from slavery, write down your response to God for His willingness to send His Son, Jesus, to save you from your sin.

The same night that brought the deepest joy for the people of Israel was a night of bitter grief and mourning for the people of Egypt. The difference between the two was the blood. Oh, how precious is the blood, that precious blood of the perfect Lamb!

For years to come, each time the people of Israel sat down to celebrate the Passover meal, their minds wandered to the goodness of God, who rescued His people from slavery through the shedding of the blood of the lamb. Each time the people of Israel tasted the lamb, they experienced anew this precious gift that God had so lovingly given them.

Have you experienced God's goodness too?

Let's Make This Personal

♦ Have you ever received the gift of the shed blood of Jesus as a sacrifice for your sin? When was the last time you celebrated the preciousness of this gift?

Today's Take Home Point

While every aspect of the Passover
table has deep significance, the whole
meal hinges on the Lamb of God, whose
blood was shed for you and me.

Final Thought

As you think about how deeply dependent the people of Israel were on God the night of the Passover meal, consider where in your life God might be inviting you to live in deeper dependence on Him.

Celebrate Good

As you consider our time in God's Word, write down one good thing you can celebrate in your life today.

Day 4: In the Aftermath

Reading: Exodus 12:29–42

Theme: God is good even when bad things happen.

For the people of Egypt, the Passover night brought the worst thing that could happen. But for the people of Israel, there was no greater sign of God's goodness than that night when the angel of God passed over the homes of those who were protected by the blood of the lamb. Think about the magnitude of that night. The king of Egypt could have prevented that disaster from happening simply by bending his knee to the Lord, but his stubbornness cost him a lot that night—and it cost his people too.

We spent most of our time yesterday focused on the lamb. Today, we're going to continue meditating on God's goodness. Is God good when bad things happen to people? Whose fault was it that so many people died on that night? Could things have turned out differently for the people of the land? Today, we're going to reflect on the aftermath of our decisions.

You and I make decisions daily that we think are inconsequential. While some of our yeses and noes might not have immense implications, some certainly do! We need wisdom when making decisions. As you ask the Lord to open your heart to His Word and will right now, ask Him for wisdom to make the right decisions.

Read Exodus 12:29–37. Write some of the words and phrases that describe the mood of the Egyptians on the night of the Passover.

In Exodus 12:30 we're told, "There was not a house where someone was not dead." Think about it. Everyone suffered that night. Every family had a bitter loss.

📍 How would you explain to the people of Egypt on the morning after the Passover the notion that God is good?

Most people struggle with believing in the goodness of God when they witness pain in the world. But let's think about what led the people of Egypt to their disaster.

📍 Review Exodus 1:8–16. What kind of a king was Pharaoh? What kind of treatment did the people of Israel have to endure at the hand of the Egyptians?

📍 Read Exodus 3:19–22. Did God already know how Pharaoh would respond to God's plan?

📍 Read Exodus 5. How would you summarize Pharaoh's heart toward God? How about the people of Egypt: How was their response to God?

◉ Read Exodus 7:13; 8:15, 19, 32; 9:12, 35. What is the common phrase in all these verses?

◉ What does it mean to have a hard heart?

God had brought nine plagues on Egypt before the Passover night. Nine opportunities for Pharaoh to soften his heart. Nine chances for the people of Egypt to turn to the Lord. Yet over and over, they refused to bend their knees to the Lord. How tragic and sad. How unnecessary the toll their stubbornness had on their future. Yet God was not surprised by Pharaoh's anger and hardened heart. In fact, you could almost say that God had a hand in it.

◉ Read Exodus 3:19; 9:12; 11:10. What is your reaction to the idea that God hardened Pharaoh's heart?

◉ Read Exodus 9:13–35. At this point in our journey, it would benefit us to spend a little extra time on this passage. First, think about the reason God hardened Pharaoh's heart. Second, think about the choice the people of Egypt had. Did some of the people of Egypt recognize God's greatness? How can you tell?

It's easy to blame God for the bad things that happen in the world. It's common to question God's goodness when tragedy strikes. But God's goodness is evident all over the world when you start looking for it. By the time the Passover meal happened, the people of Egypt had been given ample time to give their worship to the Lord. Again and again, Pharaoh refused to bow his knee to the Lord. While Pharaoh's heart turned to evil, God used Pharaoh's rebellion to magnify His glory.

God's goodness is evident all over the world when you start looking for it.

But there was an even greater reason for the necessity of Pharaoh's rejection of God. Ultimately, though Pharaoh was a major player in the story of the first Passover, the redemption story that took place on that night was far bigger than him.

All along, the Passover meal was meant to be a precursor for a far more important sacrifice that was still to come. It was vital for the lamb to be slain on the night of the Passover in order to point toward the One who would one day come to sacrifice His life for the world! Although the blood of the lamb spared the life of the people of Israel on the night of the Passover meal, it was the blood of Jesus—the Lamb of God—that would one day become the sacrifice that would save the world from sin.

When you think about the big plan of God to save the world, how does the Passover table reflect God's goodness—even for the people of Egypt who suffered on that fateful night?

Before we move on, there is one more thing to consider: the people of Egypt did indeed have the choice to believe God that night! As a matter of fact, some did just that.

◉ Read Exodus 12:38. Who do you think is meant by "a mixed multitude"?

On the day after the Passover meal, most of the people of Egypt stayed in Egypt. But some went with Moses toward the Promised Land. Some believed. God's plan has always been to save and redeem His people. He did it for the people of Israel who were covered by the blood of the lamb, and He's still doing it today for every man and woman who is willing to bend the knee and be delivered by the blood of the perfect Lamb of God, Jesus!

The question is: Are you willing to bend your knee to Jesus? The aftermath of your decision will echo through eternity.

Let's Make This Personal

◉ Where in your life are you refusing to bend your will to the Lord's? As you consider your heart today, would you describe it as soft toward the Lord, or are you hardened toward Him? How can you tell?

Today's Take Home Point

God is always good and willing to forgive
those who turn to Him in repentance.

Final Thought

In what area of your life might God be inviting you to soften your heart toward Him even more?

Celebrate Good

As you consider our time in God's Word, write down one good thing you can celebrate in your life today as a result of your repentance.

Day 5: A Movable Feast

Reading: Exodus 12:14–28

Theme: God's goodness must be practiced to be remembered.

If there is one thing common to most doctors, it's that we eat fast. You should know by now from the videos that I do everything fast, but I also eat especially fast. It was during my residency that I learned that some meals are less about being savored and more about making room for other important things—like saving lives.

The Passover table is that sort of meal. It's fast! If you've ever been invited to celebrate a traditional Passover meal, odds are you took your time eating it and enjoyed the fellowship around the table with your loved ones. You probably used the meal as an opportunity to deepen your understanding of who God is and to rejoice in all that God accomplished through the Passover. But back in Exodus 12, the people ate their meals with a quick exit in mind.

Have you ever wondered why the bread the people of Israel had at the Passover was unleavened? It's because they didn't have time to wait for it to rise! They had to take it "to go"! There was urgency in leaving Egypt and heading toward the Promised Land.

The Passover meal became symbolic of all that was still in the future for the people of Israel. Every detail of the Passover meal was meant to celebrate the goodness of God for generations to come. We're going to spend our time today focused on the importance of establishing God-given habits to celebrate His goodness in our lives.

Read Exodus 12:14–20. There were a couple of reasons that God instructed the bread to be unleavened. Can you think about what these might be? Hint: read 1 Corinthians 5:6–8, Galatians 5:9, and Matthew 16:11 for help.

In the Bible, leaven is almost always symbolic of sin. The Passover meal was more than just a meal to prepare the people of Israel for the journey ahead. It was a meal with meaning.

It was a meal about the sacrifice of a perfect lamb but also about leaving Egypt with all of its worldliness and sinfulness.

📍 As you consider your own walk with Jesus, what are some of the sinful places you left behind after turning your life to Him?

You can't walk toward the Promised Land and simultaneously stay in Egypt. You can't live for the Lord and continue living in sin at the same time. It's impossible. The importance of the unleavened bread at the Passover meal would forever be a reminder to the people of Israel of all the evil they had left behind in pursuit of the freedom they would find in the Promised Land.

📍 Read Exodus 12:21–27. God commanded His people to establish a memorial that they would observe year after year to commemorate the Passover meal. What reason were the people of Israel to give their children for the sacrifice of the lamb each year?

You can't live for the Lord and continue living in sin at the same time.

It's important to note again that the point of the Passover meal was not simply to leave Egypt. The people of Israel were also *headed* somewhere. God had promised to lead His people out of Egypt and into the Promised Land, where they could worship the Lord freely.

📍 As you consider your own journey with Christ, do you know where you're headed? Where is God leading in your journey?

The people's response to God's plan for them was awesome. Though time would reveal that their hearts were fickle, on that day of redemption, the eyes of the people of Israel saw the goodness of God clearly.

📍 Read Exodus 12:27. Write down the response of the people to God's promise of salvation.

The people of Israel were given a vivid picture of repentance through the baking of unleavened bread. They were given a picture of salvation through the blood of the lamb on the doorposts. Their response was to worship God. Slowly but surely, God was teaching His people to adopt habits and practices that would keep them tethered to His heart for years to come.

📍 What are some of the disciplines God has gifted us with to stay tethered to His heart today?

It's critical to remember all that the Lord has done for us. Despite the miracles in Egypt, including the plagues and Passover, the people of Israel would eventually forget. The Lord knew this about His people (and we're no different). It's why He established a yearly pattern for them to remember.

Q Read Exodus 13:1–16. The concept of consecrating the firstborn to God was particularly significant. What do you think the discipline of giving God the firstborn symbolized?

Q How are you honoring God in your life with the best that you have?

Picture it: The people of Israel would learn to celebrate the Passover table together year after year. God established a week every year to celebrate this table of salvation as the people of God no matter where they lived. This table became a symbol of God's goodness to His people. It became a reminder of where the people of Israel had been and a picture of how far they'd come. It also served as a reminder of all that was still to come.

Later in our study, we will spend a week studying the Lord's table (Communion), in which Christ becomes that Passover Lamb. But for centuries, the people of Israel rehearsed the goodness of God no matter where they lived and no matter what they were going through. In time, they passed on to their children this remembrance of who God is and all He had done for them. This became their legacy as the people of God and a living testimony of His goodness.

As New Testament believers, we no longer need to celebrate the Passover table. But one thing we do desperately need to do is remember.

Q What are some of the ways that God has been good to you, and what are some of the ways that you're celebrating God and worshipping Him for His goodness to you?

Let's Make This Personal

📍 What are some of the practices you've established to celebrate God's goodness to you on a regular basis? How are you communicating His goodness to the people God has put in your life?

Today's Take Home Point

In order to embrace what's ahead, you have to be willing to let go of what needs to stay behind.

Final Thought

📍 As we wrap up this week, reflect on the idea that God is saving you from your own Egypt. How might God be inviting you to remember afresh His goodness to you at the table of His salvation?

Celebrate Good

📍 As you consider our time in God's Word, write down one good thing that's still to come in your life that you can celebrate today.

Session 2: The Table of Salvation

When I Need to Be Rescued

Exodus 12:1-14

**Watch the
session 2 video now.
The video is available at
DavidCCook.org/access,
with access code
TABLE.**

1. The Passover table was the only way to _____ from slavery.

2. The Passover table was the fulfillment of God's _____ to His people.

3. The Passover table is a picture of God's substitutionary _____.

4. The Passover table is a reminder that what fills us _____.

Video Group Discussion Questions

After watching the video, discuss the following questions in your group.

📍 The people of Israel were rescued from Egypt to go to the Promised Land. What has God rescued you from, and where are you headed with Him?

📍 What part of the Passover meal intrigued you the most? How does knowing that God is in the details change your perception of God in your own life?

📍 It took faith for each family of the people of Israel to obey God's instructions the night of the Passover. Obedience always takes faith. Where in your life is God asking you to obey His Word by faith? Are you willing to do it? Have you ever considered the cost of disobedience to God on those around you?

♀ We become what we eat. What sorts of things are you eating, spiritually speaking, and how are they affecting who you are becoming?

♀ What are some of the ways God has revealed His goodness to you through this week's study of the Passover meal?

Week 2: The Table of Unexpected Belonging—When I Deserve to Be Punished

Song of Solomon 2:4

"He brought me to the banqueting house, and his banner over me was love."

Introduction

I've never felt like I truly belonged anywhere. Always an outsider, never confident that I am indeed truly wanted.

Perhaps it's because of my background. I grew up in Beirut, Lebanon, a follower of Jesus, when most of my classmates were Muslim. I was not at the top of anyone's list for a date. I remember our first school dance. I felt like a nerd. I *was* a nerd. And when one of my classmates—a bit of a nerd himself, come to think of it—asked me to dance, I thought I'd died and gone to heaven. Except that I didn't know how to dance.

Things didn't improve much for me in the years to come. High school was hard. We moved during my senior year—not just to another city, but all the way across the Atlantic, to Green Bay, Wisconsin. Are you cringing yet?

It took a few more years—well into my adulthood—before I started feeling comfortable in my own skin. To be honest, even today as a middle-aged woman, some of my old insecurities pop up. Who am I kidding? Half the time, I still don't feel like I belong. But I've learned to hide it well.

If you've ever felt like you didn't quite belong in this world, you're going to love this week's focus. We're moving from the table of salvation to the table of unexpected belonging. We're going to join King David and a man named Mephibosheth at the table of unexpected belonging. It's one of my favorite stories in Scripture and a vivid picture of God's love for us and His longing to have us sit at His table as one of His own.

God loves us and longs to have us sit at His table as one of His own.

Our problem is that we don't really believe it. We carry so much baggage of guilt and shame and insecurity that we don't quite ever make it to God's table of belonging. We miss out on all that God has for us by standing on the fringes, hoping someone will ask us to dance.

News flash: we've already been asked to dance. A place has been reserved for us at the table, and it's up to us to say yes! Are you ready to roll this week as we journey together toward this wonderful table, God's table of unexpected belonging? I'm praying that God's unending goodness and unstoppable love free you of all that's holding you back!

Day 1: Prequel

Reading: 1 Samuel 20

Theme: Relationships are God-given gifts that have the power to shape the rest of our lives.

It was a tale of three kings—sort of. While our story this week revolves around a man named Mephibosheth, it's impossible to fully understand his story without the prequel, which takes us back to our three kings.

First, there was Saul, the first king of Israel. This was a king who looked good on the outside but was rotting on the inside. After Saul revealed himself to be a self-worshipper, God took the kingdom away from him and gave it to a man after His own heart, a shepherd boy named David. David would eventually become the greatest king of Israel, but it took a few years and a whole lot of obstacles for him to finally get there, despite God's anointing on his life.

This might be a good time to remind you that just because God is in something doesn't necessarily mean it's going to be easy. Sometimes quite the opposite is true!

King Saul had a son named Jonathan, who would have been the rightful heir to the throne were it not for God's change of direction. The drama continued to unfold. Despite the fact that Jonathan should have hated David and considered him his archenemy, Jonathan and David became best friends. Jonathan understood far more than his father, Saul, did. He understood that no one can stand against God's plans and that it's better to submit to God's ways than to fight for your own ways.

Just because God is in something doesn't necessarily mean it's going to be easy. Sometimes quite the opposite is true!

King Saul hated the fact that God had chosen David to eventually replace him. Saul was also jealous of David because he seemed to excel at everything he did. So Saul put it in his mind to kill David. It became his obsession.

But he didn't succeed because of two reasons. The first is obvious: God's plan was for David to be king, and I've already mentioned that no one can stand against God's plan. The second reason was that Jonathan protected David. Saul's son and the rightful heir to the throne protected the one who would take the crown instead. It's an incredible story and the backdrop for the rest of our week together.

Finally, the star of this week's study, Mephibosheth, was also of royal lineage. He was the son of Jonathan and the grandson of Saul. Talk about drama! And though he had royal blood in his veins, he felt nothing like royalty. More on that later.

📍 Read 1 Samuel 20:1–17. Summarize your understanding of the passage.

A pact was made between Jonathan and David. It was a covenant, a promise. Covenants were serious things in those days. They were promises meant to be kept.

📍 Does it surprise you that Jonathan sided with David against his own father and his own future? What do you think motivated him to do so?

It takes a heart that is in tune with God to choose others over self. It takes humility and wisdom to submit to God's ways, especially when they seem contrary to what's culturally expected.

○ Have you ever had a situation in your life where everyone expected you to act a certain way, but you chose God's way instead? Describe it.

It took a lot of faith in God for Jonathan to trust that David would come out victorious from this battle, because David looked anything but victorious in that moment. David had very little power, while Saul was the king of the land. David had no army and no kingdom. He simply had his God and the promise God had given him for the future.

○ Have you ever thought that God made a promise to you, but your reality is still far from the fulfillment of that promise? How does David's example and Jonathan's faith encourage you to keep on believing?

You can read the entire saga in 1 Samuel 19–21, but the long and short of it is that Saul did indeed intend to kill David. Jonathan stepped in and basically saved David's life. David did have to go on the run, but not before reiterating his promise to Jonathan.

○ Read 1 Samuel 20:35–42. Focus on the last verse. What exactly did David and Jonathan promise each other in those final moments together?

This promise is pivotal to the rest of our story. After many adventures, David would one day remember and act on the promise. David's faithfulness to the covenant he made is illustrative of God's faithfulness to fulfill His promises to us, His people, no matter how long it takes!

♀ Are you waiting on God's promises in your life right now? Take a moment and write down the promise, and ask God to give you the endurance to wait for Him to fulfill His promise to you.

Years passed after Jonathan and David parted. David hid in caves and spent some time in strongholds. Slowly but surely, David formed an army. Saul never tired of chasing after David, though. One day, in the midst of battle with another kingdom, Saul was tragically killed, along with his three sons, including Jonathan. But David's reaction to the death of Saul was not so much relief as it was grief.

♀ Read 2 Samuel 1. Does David's reaction to the death of his enemy surprise you? Why, or why not?

David was a different kind of king. He was a king who loved people and a king who kept the promises he made. He was a king who acted in unexpected ways and loved unexpected people. One recipient of David's kindness was Mephibosheth, Jonathan's son. Let's meet him.

♀ Read 2 Samuel 4:4. Write down every fact you learn about Mephibosheth here.

📍 Did Mephibosheth have reasons to hide? What might those reasons have been?

Everyone has a backstory. It was Mephibosheth's past that led him to hide. It was Mephibosheth's family of origin that contributed to his pain. In many ways, Mephibosheth was a victim in his own life, but his story was about to change.

Life is about relationships and people. The more we learn about the people God has placed around us, the more compassion we will feel for them. David understood that relationships are God-given gifts that have the power to influence the rest of our lives. While it wasn't easy for David to move in love toward Mephibosheth, his love would prove life-changing to Jonathan's son.

Are you willing to do the hard work of learning people's stories in order to show them the love of Jesus? It will take time, but it will be so worth it!

Let's Make This Personal

📍 Will you take time to ask God to open your eyes to the real story behind one person you encounter today? Another good exercise is to think about your backstory. What are the painful points in your life that are contributing to the way you react to others today?

Today's Take Home Point

When God makes you a promise, He keeps it, no matter how long it takes for it to happen.

Final Thought

As you consider the friendship between Jonathan and David, might the Lord be inviting you to get to know someone in your life even more deeply for His glory?

Celebrate Good

As you consider our time in God's Word, write down one good thing you can celebrate in your life today.

Day 2: Intentionally Kind

Reading: 2 Samuel 9

Theme: One of the most disarming and godlike acts is kindness.

About thirty years must have passed between 1 Samuel 20, when Jonathan and David made a pact together (David ascended to the throne in 1010 BC), and 2 Samuel 9, where we will spend the rest of this week's study (around 980 BC).[8]

Thirty years is a long time. By the time I was thirty, I had graduated from undergraduate school and medical school and had finished my training in both pediatrics and pediatric ER. In thirty years, most people's kids get married and have babies. In thirty years, everything can change.

I can barely remember thirty years ago. Can you? Thirty years ago, I was young and idealistic. Thirty years ago, I was twenty. Who in their right mind would hold me accountable for decisions and promises I made to myself thirty years ago?

Yet here we are in 2 Samuel 9, about to see an entire life changed because David refused to forget a promise he had made thirty years prior.

📍 Think about your own life as it was thirty years ago. What were you doing? Were you even born yet? Who were you hanging out with? Did you ever dream you'd be where you are today? Are there things you thought would've happened by now that you've given up on?

Now read 2 Samuel 9. I want you to get the full picture of the story, but our focus today will rest on just three verses.

📍 Read 2 Samuel 9:1–3. Write down the question that is listed twice in these verses.

We're making our way toward the table of unexpected belonging. But before we get there, we're going to see how it all started with an act of unexpected kindness.

One of the most disarming and godlike acts is kindness.

By this point in his life, King David was the unequivocal king of an undivided kingdom. He was loved and held in high esteem by the people. He was still a man after God's heart. He had dreamed of building a temple for God in a time of relative peace. To say that things were going well for David would be an understatement. Yet it was in the midst of this time of peace and success that David did the unthinkable: he asked a question that could have changed everything in his life.

📍 As you consider the question that David asked, what do you think could have motivated him to ask it?

📍 Practically speaking, what sort of risk was David taking in looking for the son of King Saul?

You don't have to have a military background to understand the risk that David was facing in looking for his enemy's children—or the risk those children would be facing should they make themselves known! Most normal people would expect that the house of David and the house of Saul would hold some level of animosity between them. We might even assume that there could be a desire for the new king to destroy the lineage of his enemy. But David's heart was different. David was a man after God's heart, and David had made a promise to his friend Jonathan … a promise he was not about to forget even after all those years.

📍 The Bible calls David a man after God's heart (1 Sam. 13:14). What does it mean to be a person after God's heart?

📍 Do you consider yourself to be a man or woman after God's heart? How can you tell?

While we're tracking this story literally, there is an important spiritual aspect that cannot be missed. Second Timothy 3:16 reminds us that all Scripture is breathed by God for our instruction. Not a word is included that doesn't have specific reason and intention. Throughout Scripture, God uses people and stories to illustrate to us who He is.

As we continue to focus on the story of David and Mephibosheth, keep in mind that David is a type (or foreshadowing) of Christ. His responses are an illustration of God's heart toward us. Many biblical commentators have written about this typology, including Jonathan Edwards in his writing "Types of the Messiah." Edwards wrote:

> There is yet a more remarkable, manifest and manifold agreement between the things said of David in his history and the things said of the Messiah in the prophecies. His name, David, signifies beloved, as the prophecies do represent

the Messiah as in a peculiar and transcendent manner the beloved of God. David was God's elect in an eminent manner. Saul was the king whom the people chose (1 Samuel 8:18 and 1 Samuel 12:13). But David was the king whom God chose, one whom he found and pitched upon according to his own mind, without any concern of man in the affair and contrary to what men would have chosen. When Jesse caused all his elder sons to pass before Samuel, God said concerning one and another of them, "The Lord hath not chosen this, neither hath the Lord chosen this," etc. [1 Samuel 16:8–10].[9]

In thinking about David, one cannot ignore the spiritual implications for us about Jesus.

Read 2 Samuel 9:1–3 again. As you consider the spiritual implications of this typology between David and Jesus, how does David's question impact you more personally?

There is something astounding about intentional, unsolicited kindness. At this point in the story, Mephibosheth had done nothing to earn David's favor. He had no legacy to impress David with. He had no connections that would endear him to David. If anything, it was quite the opposite. Yet it was in this baffling dynamic that David asked the most unexpected question: "Is there still someone of the house of Saul that I may show the kindness of God to him?"

Has anyone ever shown you intentional, unexpected kindness? How did you react?

Unexpected kindness is disarming, isn't it? When someone surprises us with such kindness, it's almost easier to flee or fight than to receive it. It's natural to doubt the sincerity of the one extending the kindness. I tend to become suspicious when someone is kind to me. Yet we're told in Romans 2:4 that it is the kindness of God that leads us to repentance.

Try to define kindness here.

♥ As you consider your own journey with God, what are some practical ways that you've experienced God's kindness to you?

Our world today is unkind. Yet few things are more Christlike than kindness. David's kindness was born out of love. David had made a promise to his friend Jonathan, whom he loved—a promise he had not forgotten.

♥ Read Titus 3:5 as we conclude today's time together. How does the gospel message, as summarized here by Paul, reflect God's kindness to an undeserving people?

While we might be studying the story of David and Mephibosheth, I wonder if what God is trying to tell us about His goodness and His love is far deeper and greater than just the story of three kings.

Let's Make This Personal

● Who in your life are you showing unexpected and intentional kindness to? Think about the most difficult relationships in your life and how unexpected kindness from you might disarm that person and bring about healing.

Today's Take Home Point

Many happy endings start with a step of unexpected kindness toward someone who might deserve it the least.

Final Thought

● As you consider God's kindness leading to repentance, how might God be inviting you into a closer walk with Him through repentance?

Celebrate Good

● As you consider our time in God's Word, write down one good thing you can celebrate in your life today.

Day 3: Hiding in Shame

Reading: 2 Samuel 9:1–8

Theme: God wants so much more for us than a lifetime of hiding in shame.

I have a confession to make. I'm a little ashamed to share this with you, given the title of this Bible study and my attention to food. But we're already too far into this study for you to quit, so here goes: I don't cook.

My mom cooks, and just about every woman from my culture cooks. But the cooking gene was mutated in my DNA. I am, on the other hand, one of the best food and restaurant critics of all time.

Yet even I, with my paltry cooking abilities, know that a feast doesn't put itself together. It takes preparation. It takes effort. It takes tiny little steps to finally make it to the big table.

We're on our way this week to the table of unexpected belonging, and each day's homework is another step in our meal-making process. Today, we're going to focus on shame and what often keeps us hiding from the table set up for us.

Remember that while our story is focused on a man named Mephibosheth and his father's best friend, King David, this story is really about us. It's about God's love for us. It's about what happens after we feast at the table of salvation. What often happens after salvation is that we sink back into shame because our past haunts us. But God wants so much more for us than a lifetime of shame.

Read 2 Samuel 9:3–8. How did Ziba describe Mephibosheth?

What kind of emotions might have been going through Mephibosheth when David called him to his presence?

Can you imagine it? For almost thirty years, Mephibosheth, the crippled son of Jonathan, hid in shame in a town called Lo-debar. They say there is meaning in every name. I found this interesting about the town Mephibosheth was hiding in.

It turns out that the name of the town is derived from the Hebrew *debar*, which means "thing" or "word"—plus the negation *lo*, which means "no." Thus, the term *Lo-debar* would mean "nothing."[10]

> The town's name is not complimentary. The name may or may not have been an apt description of the town. If it was an apt description, it may have been lacking good pasture, or it may have been an insignificant, "nothing town." In English we might say that it was "in the middle of nowhere."[11]

Poor guy. We looked at 2 Samuel 4:4 earlier this week, and you might want to look it up again. Through no fault of his own, Mephibosheth, at the innocent age of five, was dropped by his babysitter and became crippled. To be disabled is hard anywhere, anytime in our world, but in 980 BC, it would have been much harder than it is now. There were no medical and social services to accommodate the disabled. There were no job opportunities or funding to help sustain the lives of the disabled.

Poor Mephibosheth had spent his life at the mercy of the kindness and loyalty of Ziba, the servant in a town in the middle of nowhere. His whole life had rested on the hope that no one would ever find him. His whole life had rested on the prayer that *David* would never find him. As hard as his life had been to that point, only one thing could be worse: to be found by King David, his family's enemy. So he hid until that fateful day when David called for him by name.

All of us hide in one way or another. As you meditate on the life of Mephibosheth, think about your life. Where in your life might you be hiding, or who might you be hiding from?

One of the ways we know we're hiding is to examine our fears. Mephibosheth was hiding from David because he was afraid of pain and of death. To be found by David could have resulted in a severe punishment or even execution.

♥ What are you afraid of in your life? How might you be hiding because of your fears?

We're all afraid of something. We're afraid of rejection, so we hide our real selves from others and avoid intimacy. We're afraid of losing, so we hide by not participating. We're afraid of failing, so we hide by never even trying. We're afraid of disappointment, so we never get our hopes up. We're afraid of the future, so we stay in our past.

♥ Fear is one of the greatest plagues in the Christian life, and it can be overcome only by the perfect love of someone greater than our fears. Let's reflect on these verses about fear. For each verse, write down the reason we must not fear.

   Joshua 1:9

   Psalm 23:4

   Isaiah 43:1

   Romans 8:38–39

2 Timothy 1:7

1 John 4:18

Only God's love has the power to overcome our fears. God's love has the power to find us in our darkest hiding places. God's love has the power to free us from our shame.

🔍 Read 2 Samuel 9:8. How much value did Mephibosheth believe he brought to the world?

We tend to equate our value with our accomplishments, but God values us not because of what we do but because of who we are. We tend to think that we're good enough when we've done enough, but God knows that we'll never be "good enough"—we'll only be loved enough! We are created perfectly in God's image, even when we see ourselves as imperfect.

🔍 Read Psalm 139:14. Does this verse apply only to those that society has deemed "beautiful," or to everyone?

> We think we're good enough when we've
> done enough, but God knows we'll never be
> "good enough"—we'll only be loved enough!

We are quick to write down the answers but slower to apply these truths to our own lives. We think we matter to God because of what we do for Him. God's goodness rests on the nature of who *He* is, not on how good we are. The story of David and Mephibosheth is a wonderful depiction of God's love.

You and I might feel like dead dogs. We might hide in our shame, blaming our past, unwilling to dream of a life outside of our Lo-debars. Yet God has called us by name. He invites us to His table. His goodness searches for us and stuns us with His kindness.

What an awesome God we serve!

Let's Make This Personal

What are you most ashamed of in your life? When you look at yourself, do you really believe that God loves you just the way you are? How do the words you speak about yourself reflect what you believe about God's love?

Today's Take Home Point

> It is natural to hide because of our
> fear and shame, but it's divine to step
> into the light of God's love.

Final Thought

📍 As you consider your past and your places of shame, how might God be inviting you to let go of the past and step into His love?

Celebrate Good

📍 As you consider our time in God's Word, write down one good thing you can celebrate in your life today.

Day 4: Undeserved Mercy

Reading: 2 Samuel 9:6–11

Theme: The invitation to God's table is offered out of His love and His mercy.

I'm one of those people who likes to recap a lot. I need to know where we've been, where we are, and where we're going. So … here's a recap.

We're in this Bible study to grow in our understanding of the goodness of God. In the first week of our homework, we studied God's goodness to His children through the table of salvation. The people of Israel thought they were stuck in their pain. They assumed their lot was sealed. But God came through in their wilderness of bondage and saved them with His mighty arm. He commemorated the event with a festival that would be celebrated yearly—the Passover table.

This week, we're focused on God's goodness to us when we feel we deserve it the least. We're celebrating at the table of unexpected belonging. The story of Mephibosheth is of a man who was rightfully the enemy of David. He came from a lineage of failure. He himself was crippled, though by no fault of his own. He lived in hiding at the mercy of his servant, Ziba.

The notion that David the king would invite him to sit at his table was preposterous. Most normal people would have assumed that David's intent toward Mephibosheth was evil. Instead, David was looking for a way to show kindness to Mephibosheth because of a promise David had made to his friend Jonathan. David was looking for a way to show kindness because he loved Jonathan.

It was love that motivated David to reach out to poor Mephibosheth. And it was love that motivated the Father to send His Son, Jesus, to secure a place at God's table for us.

Read Romans 5:8–10. How did Paul describe humans who have not yet accepted Jesus?

We were all once the enemies of God, separated from Him by our sin, but God in His mercy reached to us in love, offering us a new chance. God in His love offered us salvation. Today's lesson is about undeserved mercy. None of us deserves God's love, yet God lavishes His love on us through Christ. It's exactly what we read happening in 2 Samuel 9.

📍 Read 2 Samuel 9:6–11. Why did David begin his offer to Mephibosheth with the words "Do not fear"?

📍 What exactly did King David offer Mephibosheth?

Is your jaw wide open yet? David promised Mephibosheth *all that belonged to Saul and his house.* This wasn't just mercy—this was grace upon grace lavished on Mephibosheth.

Think about it! David determined to give Mephibosheth above and beyond what was expected of him. This was mind-blowing. Furthermore, we're told that Ziba and his fifteen sons and twenty servants were invited too! David meant to provide for all of them, not because he had to, but because he was a man who was true to his word. And he did it because of love!

📍 Read Romans 5:8 again. What was it that motivated God to send Jesus to die for our sin?

◉ Read 1 John 3:1. Again, what is God's motivation in the story of our salvation?

It all boils down to love and a promise. God's goodness is best understood as an extension of who He is: God is love!

God's promise to send His Son to save us from our sin was first hinted at in Genesis 3:15 in the aftermath of the fall of mankind. Then in His first encounter with Abraham (Gen. 12), God reiterated His promise to send a deliverer. In Exodus, we learn how the perfect lamb of God became a substitutionary atonement for the sin of the people—and the only way out of Egypt and into the Promised Land. Despite years in which the people were waiting, God kept His promise to send His Son to save the world, and He did it because of love.

◉ Can you now see more clearly the storyline of salvation and redemption in the story of David and Mephibosheth? Describe your understanding of it.

◉ Read Titus 3:4–7. What reason are we given for our salvation?

God's goodness is best understood as an extension of who He is: God is love!

David's offer to Mephibosheth was above and beyond what Mephibosheth could have imagined. He showed up that fateful day, possibly expecting to die. Instead, he was given life and a future. He was given hope where he expected pain.

But there was one more step for Mephibosheth to take.

📍 Read 2 Samuel 9:11. What step was necessary for David's gift to take effect?

A gift always requires a response, doesn't it? Despite David's generous offer and his mind-boggling provision, the gift had to be accepted. Mephibosheth's response was to say yes.

📍 What are some reasons Mephibosheth might have rejected David's gift?

📍 What do you think might have happened if Mephibosheth had rejected David's gift?

It's sad, isn't it, that goodness can be so easily rejected? Even though Mephibosheth said yes, many today reject the gospel message. Faced with the offer of salvation through the perfect sacrifice of Jesus, many today continue to walk away from Christ's love. Instead of the life, hope, and future they could have, they reject God's love, an act that always leads to death. Instead of a life full of joy, many choose to stay in hiding, unwilling to risk stepping into the light.

♥ Can you think of anyone in your life right now who has refused God's lavish offer of life? What do you suspect might be standing in their way?

Before we wrap up today's lesson, let's go back to where David offered Mephibosheth *all that belonged to Saul*. If there ever was a better picture of God's lavish love for us, I can't think of it.

♥ Read Ephesians 1:7–10. What are some of the blessings that God has lavished on us through salvation?

Let's end our time in praise. As we reflect on all God still has in store for us, write down a few words of praise, thanking God for who He is and what He has done for us.

Let's Make This Personal

📍 What are some of the reasons that might be keeping you from receiving God's undeserved mercy for you in this season of your life?

Today's Take Home Point

> Mercy is never deserved but always desired, and the key to unlocking mercy is simply to receive it.

Final Thought

📍 As you consider the story of David and Mephibosheth, in what specific area of your life might God be inviting you to believe in Him more?

Celebrate Good

📍 As you consider our time in God's Word, write down one good thing God has given you through Christ that you can celebrate in your life today.

Day 5: Forever Belonging

Reading: 2 Samuel 9:9–13

Theme: It's only when you embrace your new identity that you'll take your place at the table of the King.

The problem with most of us is that we receive the gift of salvation but we continue to wrestle with accepting and receiving God's grace. We struggle with showing up to God's table of belonging even though we've been lovingly invited to it. We have a hard time truly believing that despite God's invitation, He doesn't see us as His worst mistakes. Despite being invited into the light, many of us still long to hide in the darkness. It ought not be this way.

My prayer this week is not only that God uses His Word to remind you of His lavish love for you, but also that you once and for all put aside your insecurities and your fears and take your place at the table of unexpected belonging—right where you belong!

Q Read 2 Samuel 9:11–13. Jot down the words in these verses that reinforce the idea of belonging for Mephibosheth.

Think about it. In order for Mephibosheth to live the life that was offered to him, he had to move away from Lo-debar. Remember Lo-debar, that little "no place" town in the middle of nowhere? While it served well as a place for hiding, it was no place for one who was invited to live like a king's son!

Q Where are some of the hidden and dark places you have found comfort and safety in your life despite being invited into the light?

Despite God's invitation, we insist on remaining in darkness. The book of 1 John was written for believers who were offered the light but still struggled to leave the darkness.

◉ Read 1 John 1:5–7. According to this passage, is it possible to be in the light and continue to walk in the darkness?

◉ Why do you think so many followers of Jesus split their time between light and darkness?

We sin either because we do not know God yet or because we do not really believe the reality of the invitation we've been offered. Though Mephibosheth was offered the chance to eat at the king's table, there were many reasons he might have second-guessed himself. Here are a few that might have crossed his mind:

- I'm not good enough to eat at that table at all, much less daily.
- I'm not sure I really understood the invitation clearly.
- I'm embarrassed to show up to the table with my deformities.
- What if someone kills me when they find out who I really am?
- What if it's a trick to lure me to my death?
- What if I don't like the food at the king's table?

Okay, the last one sounds ridiculous, but many Christians do wonder whether life in the Father's house will measure up to the fun they are currently having in the world. The list goes on and on.

C. S. Lewis summarized it well:

> It would seem that Our Lord finds our desires not too strong, but too weak.
> We are half-hearted creatures, fooling about with drink and sex and ambi-
> tion when infinite joy is offered us, like an ignorant child who wants to go on
> making mud pies in a slum because he cannot imagine what is meant by the
> offer of a holiday at the sea. We are far too easily pleased.[12]

We are far too easily pleased. We settle for less than God has for us, and we do so for a number of reasons.

♀ What are some of the most common reasons you have used to refuse to feast at the table of unexpected belonging?

It seems too good to be true to believe that we belong at the table of the King. It boils down to a matter of identity. As long as Mephibosheth saw himself as the son of Saul, he would forever doubt the goodness and kindness of David. In order for Mephibosheth to make his way to the table, he had to let go of his old identity and embrace his new identity offered to him by the king.

♀ Read 2 Samuel 9:11. "So Mephibosheth ate at David's table _____." Fill in the blank in the space below.

"Like one of the king's sons." This lame son of Jonathan was given a whole new identity. In David's eyes, and the eyes of everyone sitting at that table, Mephibosheth was no longer the crippled grandson of Saul. He was now considered like one of the king's sons.

◆ Read 1 John 3:1. What identity does God's Word say we are given?

◆ Read 2 Corinthians 5:17. This is the first Bible verse I ever memorized. What are some things you identified with before Christ that are no longer part of the new you?

Most of us tend to think of identity superficially. For example, before we came to Christ, we might think that life is full of sex, drugs, and rock 'n' roll. But the truth is that our identity is much deeper than the things that we do or don't do. Our identity is the essence of who we are. In Christ, we have been given entirely new spiritual DNA, thereby changing our identity from the inside out. We are no longer merely our sexuality, our habits, or our preferences. In Christ, we have been made radically and completely new.

> ## It's only when you embrace your new identity that you'll take your place at the table of the King.

Because of who we have become, our actions will inevitably change. Christianity is not about behavior modification but heart change. Our actions are merely a reflection of who we believe we are. Let's reflect on our new identity in Christ as we meditate on these verses.

📍 For each verse, write down who you are in Christ:

Romans 5:17

1 Corinthians 1:2–3

Ephesians 1:6

Ephesians 2:1–5

Ephesians 2:10

Wow! It changes everything in your life when you start seeing yourself as God sees you! It changes where you live and it changes what you do. The last verse in our passage this week captures it all so well. In case you missed the answers, check out the endnote my assistant, Irina, created for you.[13]

📍 Read 2 Samuel 9:13. What goes through your mind as you picture this scene?

On the outside, Mephibosheth still looked like a man with a limp, but where it mattered the most, in his heart, he was a radically changed person. He was a son of the king! What a feast it must have been to sit at the table of unexpected belonging, not merely as a guest, but as one who belonged to the king!

Let's Make This Personal

How do you see yourself? Do your daily actions reflect what you believe about who you really are?

Today's Take Home Point

We step up to the table of belonging
not because we feel we belong but
because we've been told the truth about
who we really are and believe it!

Final Thought

How might God be inviting you to shuffle closer to your seat at the table of belonging even when you might not feel like you belong?

Celebrate Good

As you consider our time in God's Word, write down one good thing about your new identity that you can celebrate in your life today.

Session 3: The Table of Unexpected Belonging

When I Deserve to Be Punished

2 Samuel 9:1–13

Watch the
session 3 video now.
The video is available at
DavidCCook.org/access,
with access code
TABLE.

1. When I'm hiding in shame, God calls me _____.

2. When I'm too scared to be seen, God sees me completely and still _____
_____.

3. When I expect to be punished, God surprises me with His unexpected _____.

4. When I see myself as an outsider, God sees me as _____.

Video Group Discussion Questions

After watching the video, discuss the following questions in your group.

♀ What aspect of the story of Mephibosheth moved you the most?

♀ There are some things about our lives and our pasts that we can't change, so we try to hide them. Where in your life are you tempted to hide? Have you found peace in hiding?

♀ Share a specific time in your life when God astounded you with His unexpected goodness.

♀ How has your life been transformed by God's invitation to join Him at His table?

♀ What might change in your life if you started to see yourself as God sees you?

Week 3: The Table of Overflowing Satisfaction— When All I Have Is Empty

Isaiah 55:1

"Come, everyone who thirsts, come to the waters; and he who has no money, come, buy and eat! Come, buy wine and milk without money and without price."

Introduction

Why are there so many grumpy Christians? Despite what we know about the gospel and despite the fact that the gospel is called "good news," most Christians, myself included, miss the abundant joy that's ours the moment we get saved. We walk around bearing a closer similarity to Statler and Waldorf from *The Muppet Show* (they are the two old, cantankerous guys) than we do Jesus. We've taken on an Eeyore-like countenance, convinced that the world is going to fall on our heads. It ought not be that way.

This week, we're going to continue our focus on God's goodness at the table of overflowing satisfaction. This time, our passage will be short, but the lessons will carry us a long way. We will get a good glimpse at what Jesus thinks about our joy. After all, Jesus chose the most joyous occasion for His first miracle—a wedding!

This week's lessons will press us toward deeper joy. No longer do we need to carry our sourpuss identity of the worried and the burdened. This week, we're going to let go of anxiety and embrace joy. We're going to let go of sadness and practice celebrating. We're going to evaluate all the empty spaces in our lives and fight for joy.

No matter what you're going through this week, the miracle of Jesus turning water into wine—at a wedding of all places—should be enough motivation to rejoice despite your circumstances. Here's the thing about weddings: they're joyful. I've been to big weddings and small weddings, American weddings and Lebanese weddings, rich weddings and poor weddings, and the one thing they have in common is joy.

> No longer do we need to carry our sourpuss identity of the worried and the burdened. We're going to let go of anxiety and embrace joy.

Joy may be the last thing on your mind right now. You might be burdened with trials and encumbered with care. All this talk about God's goodness might strike you as a concept for someone else living a different life than yours. Trust me, I'm that person too. I'm always the one wondering how I missed the happiness stop on the train to abundant life. But I'm learning that Jesus is so committed to my joy—and yours—that He is willing to do the unexpected in order to get my attention.

I might have expected a hospital to be the location of Jesus' first miracle. Instead, God chose a wedding celebration. I mean, if you can't find joy at a wedding, what hope do you have, right? We serve a God who sees things so differently than we do. His point of view is so much broader.

My first visit to the Grand Canyon was a little underwhelming—until I took a helicopter tour and got my first real view of the southern rim. Likewise, you might be focused on the one angle in your life that feels depressing. This week's lesson will help you step back and get a God-sized view of all the Father intends for us, both now and forevermore.

We serve a God who is good and a God who takes joy in our joy. Let's get to know Him better together!

Day 1: Why a Wedding?

Reading: John 2:1–11

Theme: There are no accidents in God's economy; everything He does has a purpose.

Of all the places in the world where Jesus could have launched His ministry, He chose a wedding! Why a wedding? Why would Jesus use such a "human" event as a wedding to launch the public ministry of the Lord of all and God of the universe? Perhaps there was no more perfect of a location.

We tend to think of marriage as something from a Hollywood movie: the epitome of perfection. We imagine that marriage was created by God to fulfill us and satisfy us completely here on earth. It's why so many of us are walking around with our heads hung. If you're single, the idea of marriage as the apex of happiness can be depressing. And if you're in a bad marriage, the idea that marriage is the pinnacle of happiness can be even more depressing.

But what if there was more to marriage? What if marriage wasn't created to make us happy but to point toward something even better? In choosing a wedding feast as the place for His first miracle, Jesus relayed a message to us about who He is and what He had come to do. In choosing a wedding feast as the place of His first miracle, Jesus might be declaring to a watching world that even an earthly marriage won't bring you the joy that only the Savior can bring.

Has it ever surprised you that Jesus would choose a wedding for His first miracle? What might you have chosen instead?

From the moment that God brought Eve to Adam, the Scriptures begin to paint a narrative that is not completed at a human altar of wedding vows but in an eternal marriage between a bride and a groom. God uses an entire book in the Bible, the book of Hosea, to explain exactly how this union will play out and to show His people just how far His goodness extends.

When you stop and think about it, it should be no surprise, given all that Scripture teaches about marriage, that Jesus chose a wedding as the site of His first miracle and the launching of His ministry!

♥ Read Ephesians 5:25–27. What do these verses tell us about the relationship between Christ and the church?

♥ Read 2 Corinthians 11:2. How does God feel about the church?

♥ Read Revelation 21:1–2. Write down in your own words what these verses mean.

We think of marriage in earthly ways, but God sees it for the bigger and more divine union it really is. Marriage is indeed a big deal to God. We will spend our last week together studying the relationship between Christ as the groom and the church as His bride. But in this week's homework, we're going to begin to understand some of the bigger themes related to Jesus and marriage.

♥ Read John 2:1–11. This is our text for the week. Jot down questions that come to your mind as you read the passage. Ask God to help you glean the answers by the end of this week's homework.

The Holy Spirit is our best teacher. While I can walk you through the details of the text and give you some insights, no teacher is more available and knowledgeable than the Holy Spirit of God, who has been given to you to illuminate your understanding of God's Word and to help you apply it in your daily life. Get in the habit of asking Him to teach you as you read God's Word for yourself.

No teacher is more available and knowledgeable to you than the Holy Spirit of God.

It was God's perfect plan to use this least likely place, a wedding, to reveal to the watching world who He is and what He had come to do. Let's break down today's story.

⚲ Who were the people involved in the miracle of John 2?

⚲ Was the request that Mary presented to Jesus reasonable? What do you think of Christ's response to Mary?

I spent years baffled by Jesus' response to Mary's request. It seemed disrespectful and abrupt, sort of like I sound when I have too much on my mind. Even more surprisingly, after telling Mary that His hour had not yet come, Jesus turned around and actually *performed* the very miracle He'd implied He wasn't going to do. Have you ever wondered if the Son of God simply changed His mind?

One of the best sermons I've heard on the miracle in this passage is called "Lord of the Wine" by Timothy Keller.[14] In it, Keller explained what might have been happening. He suggested that perhaps the non sequitur came because Jesus' mind was elsewhere. Perhaps in the moment when Mary asked Jesus to perform a miracle for the bride and groom, Jesus' mind had wandered to another wedding: His future wedding to His bride, the church, and the immense cost it would take to get there.

With that perspective, Christ's statement makes more sense. The wedding feast Jesus was thinking about would be celebrated with a much more lavish feast at a later time, as described in Revelation 22.

Keller went on to explain that Jesus could very well have been thinking about what it would take for Him to provide wine for His own wedding feast someday. Though Mary was correct in commenting that they needed wine, Jesus' thoughts rested on the future. His own people did need wine, but that wine would be poured later, through the death of the precious Lamb of God—Christ Himself. No wonder Jesus' answer seemed pointed: His time (to die) had indeed not yet come.

⏻ As you think about marriage, do you find that your thoughts on marriage are influenced more by culture or by Scripture?

We've been mapping the footsteps of God throughout Scripture, focusing on God's goodness at various tables. When we get to our last week together, we will celebrate at the eternal wedding feast. One of our goals for the current week is to build on this picture of Christ as the groom and the church as His bride. While we study Christ sipping wine at the joyful wedding of a local couple, let's keep in mind that His thoughts were already moving ahead to the future, where He would spill His own blood as a sacrifice for our sins so that we could one day sit in our own sorrows, sipping the wine of coming joy.

Every word of God has purpose. Every story in Scripture is there for a reason. While we will spend this week exploring joy at a wedding in Cana, let's keep in mind that every detail we're given serves the greater purpose of fulfilling our joy in Christ as we more fully understand the extent and length of His goodness to us.

Let's Make This Personal

📍 Have you ever been tempted to reach the wrong conclusions about God based on His answers to your requests? How does today's reading change your perception of God's answers to your requests?

Today's Take Home Point

> It's easy to misunderstand Christ's response to our requests and to forget that Christ always has more in mind than just our present situation.

Final Thought

📍 With Mary's request to Jesus and His response to her in mind, what might God's invitation be to you as you consider your own prayer needs?

Celebrate Good

📍 As you consider our time in God's Word, write down one good thing you can celebrate in your life today.

Day 2: Lord of the Feasts

Reading: John 2:1–12

Theme: Christianity isn't an exercise in knowing but an experience in delighting.

One reason people turn away from Christ or delay coming to Him is that they assume the Christian walk is somber, boring, or too restrictive. Ask most young men and women who grew up in Christian homes why they left the church the moment they moved out of their parents' houses, and they will tell you that it's because they wanted to have fun. Admit it: many of us tend to think of Christianity as a goody-two-shoes, "toe the line or you're out" sort of life. It sounds boring even to me when I put it that way.

The truth about Christianity is far from that. Just look at how the Savior lived! It was God who created food for us to enjoy and who set a table for His people in the wilderness. It was God who established the practice of celebrating feasts. He even established the Feast of Jubilee, which was meant to last an entire year. In the New Testament, we see that Jesus, the Son of God, was even accused of partying too much! I'm so glad Jesus chose a marriage feast to be the setting for His first miracle. What better reminder to us that God cares about our joy. He is indeed the Lord of the feasts!

Furthermore, by turning the water into wine, Jesus stepped into the wedding ceremony as the master of the feast. It was the job of the master of the feast to make sure that the wine would not run out. For His very first miracle, Jesus turned about 150 gallons of water into wine! This wasn't a small feat. It was massive, and it told a massive story about who God is. Jesus revealed that He was the true master of the feast and has been from the very beginning.

When you think about Jesus as the Son of God, do you tend to think of Him as somber or as Lord of the feast? What has influenced your thoughts on this?

♀ Read Isaiah 25:6. What does God's Word say the Lord will prepare for His people someday?

♀ Read Jeremiah 31:10–14. Describe the scene that God paints for His children.

♀ What are some of the lessons you might conclude based on the fact that Jesus chose to turn water into wine as His first miraculous act?

Joy! Rejoicing! Happiness! Fulfillment! Abundant satisfaction! Miraculous provision even in the small things! Utter delight in the things that matter to His people! Did I mention joy? It seems as if Jesus is describing to anyone who is watching exactly what His kingdom looks like. So why are so many of God's people walking around with the cares of the world on their shoulders?

♀ How would people describe you if they interacted with you regularly but didn't know what you believed?

📍 Where in your life do you lack joy? Does knowing that Jesus cares about His people enough to turn water into wine at a family wedding change your willingness to turn to Him in your moment of need?

I've written a lot about suffering over the last couple of decades. I've published several books that help Christians understand how to make the most of suffering and how to grow through pain. I believe many of us are quite practiced in the art of suffering—and have been given ample opportunity to do so. But when it comes to joy, many of us are rusty. When it comes to joy, many of us have forgotten that we serve a Savior who has declared Himself the Lord of the feasts.

📍 What are some ways you can learn to practice joy in your life on a consistent basis?

When my nephew Sam was not yet five, he picked up the concept of "feast" somewhere, perhaps at one of the big holidays where we ate a big meal and called it a feast. Pretty soon, he applied it everywhere. If the table was set, he would say a feast was in order. He used to get on the phone and invite me over to dinner on a weeknight, informing me that we would be having a feast that night. It was endearing, and a lot closer to how all of us who follow Jesus should be living.

Christianity isn't an exercise in knowing but an experience in delighting.

Somewhere in our Christian walk, we've lost the awe that comes from recognizing that our God has set a table for us in the wilderness of life. We've lost the joy of knowing Jesus.

📍 Read Psalm 34:8. Do you notice the different senses that God instructs us to use when thinking about His goodness?

Our Christian faith is not merely one of intellectual assent. While our minds are essential in understanding the gospel, our relationship with Christ is a powerful experience for our senses too.

In the Psalms, David asks God to open his eyes to see more clearly. He invites others to taste and see that the Lord is good. The invitation we're given is to fully experience the supernatural by fully experiencing the goodness of God. Most of us know that God is good, but it is usually the sensory experience of our hearts that moves us to worship Jesus and stand in awe of who He is each time we pull up a chair to sit at the table He's provided for us—whether it be a regular weeknight meal or a Thanksgiving feast.

📍 Describe your experience with God. Has your relationship with Him been merely intellectual, or are you experiencing Him with all your senses?

The Bible presses us past just knowing about God to feasting on the Lord. God invites us to feast with Him. His Son, Jesus, chose a wedding feast to remind us that He is indeed Lord of the feasts! His goodness overflows. The creation around us reflects it with its lush valleys and mountains. The animals declare it with their various sounds and pitches. The foods we eat remind us that in the same way we savor the flavors of every meal, our experience with the Lord ought to delight and transform us as we taste of His goodness daily.

Our Christian faith is not a membership in an organization or an agreement to a way of living. It is an invitation to a feast. On more than one occasion, Jesus Himself told parables about marriage feasts to illustrate the kingdom of God.

Do you long for a fresh experience with God that leaves you utterly satisfied yet longing for even more of His goodness? Have no fear. That's exactly the kind of experience Christ has invited you to!

Let's Make This Personal

What are some of the main reasons your joy is stifled in your Christian life? What can you change so that you might delight in Christ, starting right now?

Today's Take Home Point

You can know all you want about Christianity, but it's your experience with God and His goodness that will ultimately delight and change you.

Final Thought

Since Jesus is Lord of the feast, how might God be inviting you to let go of your own expectations and beliefs in order to join Him in joy?

Celebrate Good

As you consider our time in God's Word, write down one good thing you can celebrate in your life today.

Day 3: Empty Spaces

Reading: John 2:6–11

Theme: It is only when you offer God your empty spaces that He will fill them.

As we dig deeper into the context of this week's story in John 2, it is important to know some basic facts about weddings in Jesus' day.

In Jewish society, marriage was preceded by a betrothal, which was a much more serious matter than is an engagement in our culture. The parents of the betrothed generally drew up a contract, which solemnly pledged the couple to each other. To break it was so serious that divorce proceedings were necessary.[15] The bride and groom would meet, perhaps for the first time, when this contract was signed.

The couple was considered married at this point, but they would stay separate until the time of the wedding ceremony. The bride would remain with her parents, while the groom would prepare the home that would be theirs after the wedding. This phase could take quite a while. When the home was ready, the groom would come for his bride. The marriage ceremony would then take place, and the wedding banquet would be held at the groom's house.[16]

The wedding banquet was considered one of the most joyous occasions in Jewish life and could last for up to a week. It was paid for by the groom, and any mishap at the wedding celebration would be a horrible embarrassment to the groom's family, a major faux pas.[17]

On the occasion of this particular wedding feast, Mary went to Jesus with a need that seems inconsequential compared to the problems in our world. Yet for that family, on that occasion, in that town, their problem was a pretty big deal. What a wonderful reminder for us that we can go to Jesus with every little thing we need, even if it seems small compared to the suffering in the world.

We've also been learning that the point of the miracle was not just to save the groom and his family the embarrassment of a social gaffe, but it was also a declaration of who Jesus is. In establishing Himself as the Lord of the feasts, Jesus was pointing to a future feast where His people (that's us!) will celebrate with Him forever.

In our time together today, we're going to focus on the empty jars that Jesus filled with new wine. I'm praying that God will fill empty spaces in your life as you look to Him for filling.

Read John 2:6–11. Describe the jars that were used to set up the miracle.

The stone jars that were used are referred to as a *krater* or a *kalal*, which are Aramaic words used to denote a large stone jar for ritual washing. Each jar measured twenty-six to thirty-two inches high, sixteen to twenty inches in diameter, and could hold twenty to thirty gallons of water. These were the sort of jars usually used for ceremonial washing before entering the Temple. The primary purpose of these washing rituals was to become spiritually clean and holy. In the context of wedding feasts, the jars were used to wash the guests' hands and certain utensils.[18]

Read John 2:7. Why do you think Jesus told the servants to fill the jars with water?

There were many ways to provide wine for the wedding guests. Jesus could have simply spoken wine into existence. He could have filled empty jars with new wine. But Jesus intentionally first filled the jars with water and then transformed the water into wine. I'll comment more on this later.

What does it say about our Christian walk that Jesus requested the jars be filled to the brim?

⦿ What might this miracle say about Christ's desire to transform those who come to Him for cleansing?

The Christian life is about transformation. While the jars for purification were there to clean people's hands, the advent of Christ brought a total transformation of the heart. Our relationship with Jesus does not just make us better versions of our old selves—in Christ, we are made new. Remember 2 Corinthians 5:17 from earlier? God's Word tells us that in Christ we are new creatures! We are water turned into wine, completely transformed, made new in Him.

⦿ What are some obvious ways you have seen transformation in your life since giving your heart to Jesus?

We are water turned into wine, completely transformed, made new in Him.

The jars were to be filled to the brim. Every inch of each jar that was offered to Jesus was meant to be filled for His use. Too many Christians are guilty of giving God most but not all of their hearts. We want God's blessings but are unwilling to give Him everything in our lives. We give Him *almost* everything but hang on to just a little bit of our old selves—perhaps out of fear or self-preservation.

We might give God most of our lives but hang on to our sexuality, or our ambition, or our dreams of a successful career. We might give God our lives but hang on to the stuff we own, clinging to it like a toddler with a favorite stuffed animal, hoping the security of that toy might help them through the tough days. We're oblivious to all that God has in store for us if we could just let go of our meager security blankets, especially since they will ultimately fail to satisfy us anyway.

📍 Read Matthew 16:24–25. What does Christ teach us about following Him? Is it possible to do it in stages?

📍 What are some of the empty spaces in your life that you're still holding back from God?

It was only when the water jars were filled to the brim that Christ was able and willing to transform the water into wine. Do you long to be transformed by Jesus? Do you wonder why you're still drinking the stale water of your old life instead of fresh wine? Perhaps the answer is more obvious than you'd like to admit.

📍 What will it take for you to give God your all?

Let's Make This Personal

📍 What are the empty spaces in your life that you long to have filled? What are you hoping to be filled with? Will you trust God to fill you with fresh wine in those specific areas?

Today's Take Home Point

Most of us want the outcome of a miracle without the process of the miracle. Until you're willing to give God your all, you won't see Him transform your all.

Final Thought

📍 As we wrap up today, what might God be inviting you to let go of as you look to Him for filling?

Celebrate Good

📍 As you consider our time in God's Word, write down one good thing you can celebrate in your life today.

Day 4: Key to Breakthrough

Reading: John 2:1–8

Theme: The greatest miracle of all is believing God, no matter what.

We're feasting this week at the table of overflowing satisfaction. We're celebrating a wedding feast with Jesus. We've already spent some time at the table of salvation, when the people of Israel needed to be rescued. We spent a week at the table of unexpected belonging, celebrating with Mephibosheth the unmerited love and mercy of God to us.

This week's table is special too. It's the table of Christ's first miracle. It's a table that at first glance seems inconsequential—a family wedding in a small town in the middle of nowhere. But oh, the spiritual lessons we're gleaning from this table! Every aspect of this table is about abundance and joy. It's the kind of miracle most of us dream about in our daily lives. It's the sort of breakthrough most of us long for in our area of deepest need.

Raise your hand if you want to see a miracle in your life right now! I know I do. I long to see the miraculous in my life. I long to see God turn water into wine and move mountains in the problem areas of my life. I'm sure you do too.

In order for us to see the outcome of the miracle, we need to understand the working of the miracle. The truth is that most of us prefer a genie in a bottle, someone who will show up and do all the work without any effort on our part. The good news is that it's not effort that tips the miracle. If there is one thing we can learn about breakthrough this week, it's that the miracle isn't always in the doing … it's in the believing. Let me explain.

📍 Read John 2:1–8. Write Mary's response to Jesus in verse 5. What do you think caused her to say what she did, especially after what Jesus had said?

"Do whatever He tells you." If there is a secret sauce to breakthrough in the Christian life, Mary nailed it. Do whatever He tells you. Mary had the confidence that Jesus would act on her behalf. Even after His initial refusal, she knew her son enough to know that He always

did what was right. She had the confidence to believe Him, even before she saw the miracle happen.

Isn't that what faith is? I've heard faith defined as "believing God and acting on it no matter how I feel, knowing that God always promises a good result." Another definition I like is "faith is believing in advance what only makes sense in reverse." Whether you love or hate these definitions, ultimately, faith that rests in the goodness of God is always rewarded with the goodness of God.

Mary was at a crossroads. Her situation didn't make sense. Yet instead of walking away from Jesus in disappointment, she was willing to do the work of the miracle. She believed. More importantly, she believed Jesus! It's always the object of our faith that gives power to our faith. It's not just *that* we believe, but that we believe in the person of Christ and in His goodness. While having faith in God doesn't always ensure we receive the outcome we want, it always ensures the outcome that God knows is best!

Read Matthew 17:20. Why is this verse so difficult for Christians to practice? What are some of the reservations you might have in reading this verse?

While having faith in God doesn't always ensure we receive the outcome we want, it always ensures the outcome that God knows is best!

When Mary first approached Jesus with her request, He seemed to say no. She could have walked away in frustration. She could have argued with Him. But she did not. Instead, she urged those around her to obey whatever He asked.

◉ What have your responses been to God's denials of your prayer requests?

◉ How does Mary's example encourage you to change?

James tells us that "you do not have, because you do not ask" (James 4:2). I know it can get more complicated when we bring in our motives for wanting, but for today's discussion, let's keep things simple. We're told that we have not because we ask not.

I don't know about you, but any time I feel like God has delayed in answering my prayer requests, I'm quick to hide in a corner and lick my wounds, wondering what I did to mess things up. Perhaps Mary can teach us a thing or two about prayer.

◉ Read John 2:6–8. What did Jesus ask the servants to do?

Easy-peasy, right? Fill the jars with water. Let's turn off our twenty-first-century brains for a moment and consider what Jesus was asking. There was no running water in that home in those days. The only way to fill a jar with water was to get water from the well. And this was not just one jar to be filled, but a total of six jars of water, each potentially holding thirty gallons of water! This was a big job that demanded faith.

Still want that breakthrough in your life? The servants had never seen Jesus perform a miracle. They were to act by faith without a clue what the outcome would be. The cost for them was not minimal. It was a lot of work with the risk of looking silly when the water/wine was presented to the master of the feast. We're told that the wine was offered to the master of the feast without anyone even tasting it first! Yet they filled the jars to the brim.

♥ Consider the servants' response. Why do you think they were so willing to obey?

We don't know the reason. Perhaps they knew Mary enough to trust her, or maybe they had observed Jesus' life long enough to know that He would not ask them to do something unless it was needed. We'll never know the details this side of heaven, but there is one thing we can know for sure: it was their obedience that tipped the scales to the miraculous.

Obedience tips the scale to the miraculous! Our obedience matters. It's our faith that motivates us to obey, but ultimately, obedience tips the scales to the miraculous. I am learning that more often than not, the miraculous is less about getting what I want and more about becoming more like Christ!

♥ Are there any areas in your life that God is asking you to obey Him in and you're still refusing?

♥ If you knew that your obedience might usher in a breakthrough in your life, would you be more willing to obey?

We're a lot like children when it comes to faith. I hang out a lot with my nephew Sam. He's eight. I've lost count of how often I've asked him to do something for me. When he refuses, I bribe him with ice cream. It always works. I look forward to the day when his obedience will come more naturally, when he will trust me enough to know that obedience for the sake of obedience is good, and that obedience always ushers in peace and a blessing. But until he's old enough to learn it, I'm happy to offer him rewards for his obedience.

Too often, our problem is that we look to miracles as the main sign of God's goodness. If God gives us what we want, then He must be good. We are still childish in our approach to obedience, just like my nephew Sam can be. While the miraculous can point to the miracle maker, it's not the miraculous that proves the goodness of God. Real breakthrough happens when we finally understand that God is good even without the miraculous. I have a long way to go in this area.

Mary exemplified faith that believed God through any circumstance. I wonder if the greater miracle than the water turning into wine was the breakthrough that Mary had the moment she decided to believe the goodness of God no matter the outcome. The question is: Do you?

Let's Make This Personal

📍 Where in your life are you still waiting for a miracle? Are you willing to let go of the outcome as you continue to walk in delighted obedience, trusting God to do what's best?

Today's Take Home Point

Real breakthrough happens when you believe the goodness of God no matter the outcome.

Final Thought

📍 In what area of your life is God inviting you to trust Him more?

Celebrate Good

📍 As you consider our time in God's Word, write down one good thing you can celebrate in your life today.

Day 5: *After the Miracle*

Reading: Luke 4:16–30

Theme: God loves us not because we believe but despite the fact that we don't.

What a table we've been celebrating this week! We've been feasting at the table of overflowing satisfaction. We've spent the week studying the miracle where Jesus turned almost 150 gallons' worth of water into wine. The miracle at Cana was magnificent and significant. It was the first miracle in the life of Jesus as He launched His public ministry to the world.

Jesus was around thirty years old at the time of the miracle. He had lived all His years in Nazareth up to that point, which was situated about five miles south of Cana.[19] This was His hometown and the place where Mary and Joseph had settled. Nazareth was a small town, home to fewer than three hundred people, mostly farmers and tradesmen. It was a town where everyone knew everyone.

The people in the neighboring village of Cana most certainly knew who Jesus was as well: the son of Mary and Joseph who had been trained to be a carpenter. This was the setting God chose for the very first miracle. It was where a wedding took place that became the site where Jesus declared to a watching world who He was and what He had come to do. Many believed in Him, but not everybody did.

As we conclude this week together, we're going to look past the miracle to the aftermath of the miracle. Most of us dream of the miracle. We think that if only God would perform the miracle we long for, we'd never doubt again. We'd never fear again. We'd never *want* again. We put too much weight on the miracle and not enough weight on Jesus. We need to learn to flip the narrative: It's Jesus we need more than the miracle. It's Jesus who tips the scale toward our joy. Miracles may come and miracles may go, but it's Christ who endures forever.

Read John 2:9–11. Describe the people's reaction to the miracle.

◉ At the end of verse 11, we're told that His disciples believed Him. What do you think the rest of those watching thought?

It's Jesus we need more than the miracle. It's Jesus who tips the scale toward our joy.

If you've ever read the Gospels carefully, then you might have picked up on this theme: No matter how massive the miracle Jesus did, only some of the witnesses believed. Many still doubted. Many refused to believe the truth, even when it was evident for all to see.

◉ Do you think the disciples believed because they were chosen to be disciples, or do you think they became disciples because they believed?

That brings up the question of predestination or "election." Predestination is a fascinating concept that has divided churches and been the topic of volumes of commentaries and books over the years. While we're not going to delve into it here, it's an important concept that deserves some thought. If you're interested in reading more of what the Bible has to say about it, read Ephesians 1 and prayerfully ask the Lord to help you understand His Word more clearly.

We're told that the disciples believed and that the master of the feast was amazed. The miracle Jesus did at the wedding left an impression on everyone in that region. Even though the people in those days did not have social media, this was a story that would have made the rounds at dinner tables for weeks to come. Which makes what comes next so surprising.

Read Luke 4:16–30. How did the people of Nazareth respond to Jesus here?

Read Mark 6:1–6. What did Jesus marvel at regarding the people of Nazareth?

Only a few months had passed since the wedding when Jesus came home to Nazareth. I would think that if one of their own had performed a bona fide miracle, it would have left a deep and positive impression on the people of Nazareth. But instead of awe, they harbored anger in their hearts toward Jesus. Instead of hunger for more of God, they wanted to kill Jesus. Instead of rejoicing in the presence of Jesus, they grumbled with disdain, perhaps even wondering, *Who does this young upstart think He is?*

Does the reaction of the people of Nazareth surprise you after they had witnessed, or at least heard about, Jesus performing something miraculous?

Before casting stones at the people of Nazareth, consider your own life. Have you ever seen God answer some major prayer in your life only to later question His goodness toward you?

We are quick to forget. No matter how abundant the table of God's goodness is, we are prone to turn elsewhere for satisfaction. We long for the miraculous, but soon after we see the miraculous, we forget. Our memory, much like the memory of the people of Israel, is short.

○ How can you train yourself to remember the goodness of God in your life?

There is an interesting little section of Scripture in John 2 shortly after the account of the miracle at Cana. It's worth reading now.

○ Read John 2:23–25. What did Jesus know about people that you and I tend to forget?

It's freeing to know that Jesus knows us so well and still loves us so much. He's not surprised by our fickle hearts. He might be grieved by our hard-heartedness, but He's certainly not surprised. His love for us is the opposite of what we deserve. Despite the people of Nazareth rejecting Him and wanting to kill Him, Jesus still made the painful walk to Golgotha to lay down His life for them.

Today, you and I can rejoice at the table of God's overflowing satisfaction, not because we've earned God's love, but despite the fact that we never could!

Are you satisfied to the brim with Christ's goodness for you?

Let's Make This Personal

📍 Is there anyone in your life right now who you've been quick to condemn because of their rejection of Jesus? How does Christ's example move you to change your attitude toward that person?

Today's Take Home Point

The test of true faith comes when the miracle is over and you finally realize that even better than the miracle is the miracle maker.

Final Thought

📍 As we wrap up this week's study, how is God inviting you to feast more deeply to find your satisfaction in Him alone and not only in what He can do for you?

Celebrate Good

📍 As you consider our time in God's Word, write down one good thing you can celebrate in your life today.

Session 4: The Table of Overflowing Satisfaction

When All I Have Is Empty

John 2:1-12

Watch the session 4 video now. The video is available at DavidCCook.org/access, with access code TABLE.

1. It is only when we're faced with our _____ that we'll ask the Savior to fill us.

2. It is only as we do what Jesus _____ that we'll see Him fill our empty spaces.

3. It is only as we're willing to _____ no matter what that we will experience real breakthrough.

4. Even after we experience the miraculous, we will struggle to believe _____.

Video Group Discussion Questions

After watching the video, discuss the following questions in your group.

📍 That Jesus chose a wedding in Cana as the location for His first miracle is astounding. What are your thoughts on this surprising choice for a location?

📍 Most of us want God for what He can do for us. Do you find that to be true when you look around at Christians today? What are some ways to prevent this from happening?

📍 The picture of jars that needed to be filled to the brim speaks volumes to our need to offer Jesus our whole selves. What are some of the areas in your life that you've been tempted to hold back from Jesus?

♀ The people of Nazareth later wanted to stone Jesus. Does their reaction surprise you? What are some similarities in the culture's response to Jesus back then and the response of our culture to Jesus today?

♀ Have you found Jesus to satisfy you completely? Share some practical ways you've experienced His overflowing satisfaction in your life.

Week 4: The Table of Remembrance—When I'm Apt to Forget

John 6:35

"Jesus said to them, 'I am the bread of life; whoever comes to me shall not hunger, and whoever believes in me shall never thirst.'"

Introduction

There are many reasons we celebrate meals, but an important one is to remember. We celebrate birthdays, even after a loved one passes away, because we want to remember that person. We celebrate Thanksgiving over a turkey meal so we remember to give thanks. We celebrate the Fourth of July with brats and watermelon in order to remember our independence.

We gather around the table to celebrate graduations, anniversaries, engagements, and promotions because meals have a way of transforming our monotonous days into significant moments of remembrance. We pause in the middle of our busy lives and gather with our loved ones in order to make space for this remembrance.

We are prone to forget. We live with the glazed look of the marginally interested. We get bogged down with deadlines and overwhelmed by life's demands. We have the uncanny ability to remember the negative and gloss over the good. We rush through our days chasing an illusion.

Into that frenzied life, almost like an abrupt and unwelcome interruption, comes the necessity to participate in forced gatherings that—if we let them—will soothe our souls: birthdays, engagements, holidays, and anniversaries. We are obligated to pause in the hurry of life, and we may take the opportunity to gulp down the oxygen of joy that sustains us until the next gathering. No matter what your ethnic or family background is, I'm guessing you understand and even crave the table of remembrance.

It shouldn't surprise us by now that Jesus used a table to help us remember. Throughout the Old Testament, God used tables as life-giving places of celebration. Remember the Passover table? Every year was a celebration of life. Food became a picture of the people's dependence on the Lord. Just as our bodies need physical food, so our spirits are desperate for the spiritual food that only God can provide.

We serve a God who sets a table for His people in the wilderness. God loves to feed His children. Throughout their time in the wilderness, God fed His people daily with manna. It was both a gift in a time of hunger and a promise that there was still more to come. Year after year, the people of Israel celebrated the feast of the Passover while their eyes drifted toward the heavens in their longing for the promised Messiah. Last week, we celebrated at the table of overflowing satisfaction, where Jesus revealed more of who He is. The wine that had been water was symbolic of His blood, which would eventually be the key to our joy and salvation.

God loves to feed His children.

This week, we're going to sit at what is arguably the most important table in the whole Bible: the Lord's table. We're going to deepen our understanding of the significance of the wine as we remember all that God has done for us and still intends to do.

Though we're apt to forget, God in His goodness has made provision for us to remember—and He's done it through a table, one that reminds us that we have reason to rejoice even in the wilderness of life. I hope you're ready to dig in!

Day 1: The Last Passover

Reading: Matthew 26:17–25

Theme: The greatest act of God's provision happened at the cross.

Almost thirteen hundred years had passed since the Passover was instituted in the land of Egypt. Think about it: For thirteen hundred years, the people of Israel celebrated the Passover meal together every year. Whether they were in the wilderness or the Promised Land, in Babylonian exile or under the rule of the Roman Empire, year after year, the people would find an unblemished lamb to sacrifice in celebration of the Feast of Unleavened Bread in remembrance of God's deliverance in Egypt. They gathered to celebrate the goodness of God, though they didn't fully understand that goodness.

When John the Baptist showed up, he proclaimed the coming of the Messiah. The day he saw Jesus at the Jordan River, he declared, "Behold, the Lamb of God, who takes away the sin of the world!" (John 1:29). God's people should have connected the dots. They should have seen the signs. But just like we so often do, they missed the signs God had given them.

The point of the Passover meal was to remember not only the divine deliverance from Egypt but also the promise of a coming Messiah. The lamb was always meant to point toward the perfect Lamb of God who would once and for all take away the sins of the world. God's plan was always to provide a perfect sacrifice for sin through His perfect Son, Jesus. This brings us to the night before the crucifixion.

Read Matthew 26:17–25. What did Jesus mean when He said, "My time is at hand"?

We're told the disciples prepared the Passover meal (v. 19). Think back to week 1 and try to describe what that preparation would entail.

The disciples sat down to eat. All twelve of the disciples—including Judas—sat with Jesus at the table.

Have you ever been invited to a special event and sat down to eat only to look around and see the face of someone you wished hadn't shown up? It seems like there's always an unwanted guest at every dinner table.

📍 Read Matthew 26:20–25. Was Jesus aware of what Judas was up to? How did Jesus handle the situation?

It's interesting. If you became aware of someone's intention to harm you, you might do something about it, like confront that person or report them to the authorities. You might even make a plan to escape from them. But Jesus didn't. Jesus remained at the table without missing a beat.

📍 Read John 10:17–18. What do Jesus' words tell us about why He came to earth?

It happened often during His ministry: Jesus verbally predicted His death and tried to prepare His disciples for it too. He challenged the religious leaders and told them to destroy the Temple, promising that He would raise the Temple in three days (John 2:19). He sent His disciples to prepare this last Passover meal with a message: "My time is at hand." The same Jesus who had told Mary at the wedding in Cana that His time had not yet come now declared that His time indeed had come.

So, sitting across from Judas, knowing the exact nature of Judas' plan, Jesus dipped the bread in the bowl and ate with His disciples.

◉ Read 1 John 4:9–10. What do these verses tell you about why Jesus was willing to lay down His life at the cross?

He did it for love. For God so loved the world that He gave us His Son (John 3:16). It was love that would carry Jesus through the ordeal that lay ahead. While the people of Israel might have been lulled into thinking that an unblemished lamb could save them, Jesus, God's own Son, knew that the animal sort of lamb was only a temporary means of salvation until the perfect Lamb of God was ready to die once and for all for the sin of the world.

◉ Read Hebrews 10:9–14. Write down the difference between the lamb that was slain at Passover each year and the sacrifice of Christ for our sin.

In the account of the disciples gathering for this last Passover meal, did you notice that one thing was missing? While the meal in Matthew 26 happened during the week of Passover, there is no mention of the disciples looking for a lamb to be slain. There is no mention of any preparation for an animal sacrifice.

On the night of the Last Supper, Jesus and His disciples walked over to the Mount of Olives, and Jesus knelt to pray in the garden of Gethsemane. That was also the very same night that Caiaphas would arrest Jesus. The next day, the day of the Passover meal, Jesus would be crucified on a cross. He Himself was the perfect Lamb of God whose blood was shed once and for all for the remission of our sin. They didn't need a lamb for the meal ... because the perfect Lamb of God was already there.

📍 How does an understanding of the timeline of the last Passover meal affect your life today?

We tend to make the Bible a book about us, when it's really a book about God. Yet the more we understand God, the more we understand ourselves. The implications of God's perfect provision through the events of the Last Supper should impact us deeply. Jesus, knowing that He would be betrayed by one of His own disciples, still sat at the table and dipped His bread in the bowl. Jesus, knowing He would be abandoned by His closest friends, held no resentment or anger toward them.

We tend to make the Bible a book about us, when it's really a book about God.

His love for His people was so deep that it overshadowed any other emotion. His love *for you* is so deep that He willingly submitted Himself to the cross in order to make a way for you to the Father! Are you worried about the future? Have you been waiting for God's provision in your life? Do you wonder if God cares about your life? You can let go of your doubt, because you have a God who cares!

Let's Make This Personal

📍 Where in your life have you wondered about God's love for you? Are there details about your life that seem unnoticed by God? Are you willing to surrender your fears to God, whose love for you is unending?

Today's Take Home Point

There is not a detail in the universe that
God has not perfectly planned.

Final Thought

With Jesus' last Passover table in mind, where do you think God might be inviting you to trust Him more?

Celebrate Good

As you consider our time in God's Word, write down one good thing you can celebrate in your life today.

Day 2: The Lord's Supper

Reading: Matthew 26:26–29

Theme: God's ways are for our good even when they don't make sense to us yet.

Jesus' last Passover became the first Lord's Supper, also known as Communion. If you've been to church for any length of time, you've probably had Communion. If you had no idea what the elements of the table meant, take heart: you're going to understand them today.

The Lord's Supper is one of the main sacraments for the New Testament believer. While we don't have as many feasts in New Testament church life as they did in the Old Testament, the celebration of the Lord's table is one of the most important and joy-filled meals we've been given to celebrate what we believe!

📍 Read Matthew 26:26–29. What did the bread and the blood symbolize, according to Jesus' words?

📍 What did Jesus mean in verse 29?

There are a number of church traditions and opinions about the sharing of the bread and wine. Some teach that the bread and the wine actually become Christ's body and blood as each person consumes them. But I believe that Jesus referred to the elements of the supper as symbolic of what they stood for.

In fact, this was not the first time that Jesus had referred to Himself as the bread of life.

📍 Read John 6:35–59. Jesus was speaking metaphorically here. What deeper spiritual lesson does the manna God gave in the wilderness teach us?

📍 Read Deuteronomy 8:3. Further build on the picture of Christ as the bread of life. What are some ways that we become more hungry for God?

God humbles us and lets us hunger in order to lead us to the only source of food that will ever satisfy us: Himself!

We tend to look at hunger as a curse, whereas God often uses it as a gift. For example, I spend a lot of time doing international relief work, and I have noticed that the people groups who have the greatest physical needs are often more aware of their need for God. They are hungry for help. They are thirsty for more. Conversely, the more sated we are with the needs and superficialities of life, the less hunger for God we may feel.

The Jews were offended when Jesus referred to Himself as the bread of life. They understood exactly what Jesus was insinuating. They understood that Jesus was putting Himself in the place of God by doing so.

God's ways are for our good even when they don't make sense to us yet.

On the night before the crucifixion, Jesus transformed His last Passover into the Lord's Supper. No more would a lamb be needed as a sacrifice for sin. The bread would now symbolize Christ's body sacrificed for the salvation of people. The shedding of blood as a sacrifice for sin was always God's requirement in establishing a covenant. In the same way, Christ's blood was shed for the remission of sins (Heb. 9:22).

♀ What do you think went through the minds of the disciples as they listened to Jesus talk about His body and blood?

Just like the disciples, most of us have a hard time understanding what God is doing in our lives. We go through the motions of life with too many questions to know where to start. Sometimes we think we understand God's ways. The disciples thought they understood the events happening around them, but their actions around the time of the crucifixion revealed that they had no idea what God was up to.

One of the most important lessons in our Christian walk is to learn to trust God even when His ways don't make sense to our human understanding. As long as God knows the way, we don't need to. All He asks of us is to follow.

♀ Can you think of an area in your life that has you confused? Have you doubted God's plan for you in the midst of your confusion? Express your heart here.

Most of the people in the time of Jesus were happy that He offered them physical bread to eat in response to their hunger. They didn't complain when He miraculously fed the five thousand. It was when He offered them lasting joy and satisfaction through the sacrifice of Himself that they struggled to believe.

Not much has changed today. Most of us, even Christians, are happy so long as God gives us what we want. But what we *need* is often far better than what we want. Trusting God for what we need rather than demanding from Him what we want is the only pathway to joy.

While the lessons we glean from the Lord's table are many, perhaps none is more important than the need to trust God even when we don't understand Him. Are you willing to trust Him today?

Let's Make This Personal

Are you dependent on physical bread for your satisfaction, or are you starting to see Christ as the only bread that will satisfy you forever? What are some ways you can increase your appetite for God and His Word in your life?

Today's Take Home Point

While food might satisfy us temporarily, only Christ will satisfy us deeply and eternally.

Final Thought

♀ How might God be inviting you to taste Christ, the bread of life, even more deeply?

Celebrate Good

♀ As you consider our time in God's Word, write down one good thing you can celebrate in your life today.

Day 3: In Remembrance

Reading: 1 Corinthians 11:23–26

Theme: One of the greatest gifts God gives us is the gift of remembering.

There is no greater evidence of God's love for us than the cross where Jesus died. And there is no greater sign of His goodness to us than in the Lord's Supper, which helps us remember how deep His love for us is!

We're jumping to Paul's writings today. Though his letters follow the Gospels in the table of contents of the New Testament, it is thought that Paul wrote some of his letters, including the one we're looking at today, before any of the Gospels were written.[20] If so, then Paul's instructions in this passage are the first-recorded biblical account of the Lord's Supper.

Read 1 Corinthians 11:17–26. What do the verses leading up to the description of the Lord's Supper tell you about the spiritual condition of the Corinthian church?

The Corinthian church was dealing with sexual sin when Paul wrote to them. The Corinthian believers were bent on sinning. They had even taken what was meant to be a holy reminder and turned it into an opportunity to sin. No one needs a reminder of the gospel message more than the person who is stuck in a pattern of sin. How easily we forget the price Jesus paid for our sin. How quickly we are tempted to walk away from the preciousness of the gospel to follow our own sinful nature.

Focus on verse 23. Whose idea was it to remind the Corinthian believers of the Lord's Supper?

◉ In verses 24 and 25, what reason did Paul give to practice the Lord's Supper?

We humans are prone to forget. We forget that which matters the most.

My father passed away six years prior to when I wrote this chapter. Earlier in the day, I had a couple of conversations with my family, trying to figure out if it had been six or seven years since he had passed away. Some days, I can barely remember his face or the tone of his voice. I hate that. Some days, I'm too rushed to remember. I speed through life as if the future of the world depends on me. But forgetting can be deathly. Forgetting can slowly snuff the joy out of your life.

◉ What are some of the precious memories in your life that you don't ever want to forget? What are you doing to remember them?

Forgetting can slowly snuff the joy out of your life.

For followers of Jesus, remembering what Jesus did at the Lord's Supper is nonnegotiable.

◉ Focus on verse 26. How often, according to the Bible, does the Lord's Supper need to be practiced? And for how long?

Some churches have Communion every week. Others do it every month or once a quarter. While we're not given a specific timeline for the Lord's Supper, we are instructed to celebrate this meal of remembrance on a regular basis. We're also instructed to celebrate it until the coming of the Lord.

It's meant to remind us. It's meant to jog our memories to the biggest and most important event in our lives. It's meant to lead us to celebrate afresh the goodness of our God. This meal, more than any other, was given by God to help us remember.

📍 What are some of the precious aspects of the gospel that you're led to remember each time you eat the bread and drink the cup?

📍 How does remembering what Christ did for you on the cross impact your life right now?

Thinking about the table of remembrance might seem like a nice idea or a lofty notion, but it's much more than that. The gospel is about practical living. The gospel is about shaping our minds, softening our hearts, and sharpening our vision for life. It's about why we do what we do. It's about waking us up to the spiritual realities of our world. It's about endurance and strength. It's about standing strong and unshaken in a world that is shaking. It's about the choices we make and the attitudes we hold. It's even about the friendships that we hold so dearly.

The gospel shapes us and molds us and revives us. It transforms us and brings us back to our best, Christ-centered selves.

Tomorrow, we'll look at the necessary self-reflection that takes place as we partake of the Lord's table. Today, let's not forget what we are meant to remember. Let's celebrate the goodness of the Lord and refuse to ever forget His deep and steadfast love for us.

Let's Make This Personal

⦿ What is it that you've forgotten about the gospel? What needs to change in your life as you meditate on who God is and what He has done for you?

Today's Take Home Point

We are likely to forget what we don't
make an effort to remember.

Final Thought

⦿ As you think about the Lord's table, what is God inviting you to remember about His love for you?

Celebrate Good

⦿ As you consider our time in God's Word, write down one good thing you can celebrate in your life today.

Day 4: Self-Reflection

Reading: 1 Corinthians 11:27–34

Theme: Without regular self-reflection, we are prone to wander from holiness.

Some of my earliest church memories are of Communion. Though we grew up in Beirut, Lebanon, my family was part of a small Bible-believing local church. Once a month, I would watch my mother take the cup and hold the bread, head bowed, and prayerfully partake of this meal the Lord had given us.

Though I didn't understand much about Communion in those days, what I did recognize was the seriousness of the Lord's table. Once I gave my life to Jesus and was invited to the table too, I was taught the practice of self-reflection before eating the bread and drinking the cup.

The longer I walk with the Lord, the more I see my need for self-reflection. Sin seems to cling to me even when I want to escape it. I long for holiness but find myself tainted with worldly attitudes and selfish motives. This process of deepening awareness of sin is not a surprise to the Lord. In fact, one of the purposes of the Lord's table is to serve as an opportunity for self-reflection and repentance.

What a gift we've been given to pause on a regular basis as a body of Christ followers and be given a chance to reset. While Communion is a celebration of the entire gospel message, it also serves as a way to deepen our hunger for holiness.

📍 Read 1 Corinthians 11:27–34. What do you think it means to partake of the Lord's Supper in an unworthy manner?

📍 What did Paul warn would happen to the person who ate and drank in an unworthy manner?

We tend to undermine the holiness of God. Maybe because we live in a casual society, maybe because we aren't familiar with God's Word, or maybe even because of our arrogance, but somehow we have minimized the seriousness of the holiness of God.

Holiness includes the idea of separation. The word *holy* comes from a word meaning "to separate or cut off." In reference to God, it reflects the idea that God is separate from anything that is sinful and evil. He cannot tolerate sin. When the prophet Isaiah saw the Lord, his response to God's holiness was astounding.

Read Isaiah 6:1–5. How did Isaiah respond to God's holiness?

Even the demonic spirits were afraid of the holiness of God.

Read Mark 1:24. How did the demons address God?

One of the riches of the Lord's table is that it is a symbolic reminder of the extent to which God went to give us access to His holy presence. It was because of Jesus' broken body and spilled blood that we were given access into the holy of holies. Our ability to enter God's presence is not based on how good we are but on the price that Jesus paid for our sin. Read the following verses and write down what Jesus did for us.

2 Corinthians 5:21

Ephesians 2:18

1 Timothy 2:5–6

Hebrews 4:15–16

> Our ability to enter God's presence is
> not based on how good we are but on
> the price that Jesus paid for our sin.

The good news of the gospel rests on the fact that Jesus granted us access into the presence of a holy God. The Lord's table is a regular reminder of the gift of God's mercy.

Yet we struggle with sin. Because of our flesh and because we're still living in a world controlled by Satan, we struggle to be holy and Christlike. This too is not a surprise to our heavenly Father. In 1 John 1, God tells us exactly how to deal with our sinfulness as we continue to draw closer to the Lord and His ways.

Read 1 John 1:5–10; 2:1–2. How does John instruct us to deal with the reality of our sin?

Though we sin, we have an advocate, Jesus Christ, who is the propitiation (appeasement) for our sin. According to John, to deny that we sin is to lie. To admit our sin is the first step to forgiveness and a healthy relationship with God.

How does this tie into the Lord's Supper? As a God-given sacrament that celebrates the price Jesus paid for our freedom, this meal grants us a *reminder* of the extent God went to in order to have a relationship with us.

It's a reminder of God's holiness and our desperate need for a Savior. It's a reminder of the privilege we've been given to enjoy God's presence through Christ. It's a reminder of our humanness and our propensity to wander from God's ways. It's a reminder that we love sin and need God's mercy to let go of sin and learn to enjoy the only One who will satisfy us forever. It's a reminder that we desperately need Jesus.

Besides being simply an opportunity to remember where we've come from, the Lord's Supper is also a time to reflect about where we're going. In 1 Corinthians 11:27–32, Paul wrote some strong words about the need for us to self-reflect and examine ourselves before participating in the Lord's Supper. Each of us is instructed to reflect on his or her own self. It's easy to examine others, but what God calls us to is an inward look of confession and repentance. Anything less than an honest self-reflection is a lie.

Q What does it mean to examine yourself or reflect on your life? How do you do it?

Biblical self-reflection is an important concept. While many people in the world might refer to self-reflection as a step in knowing ourselves more deeply through introspection, biblical self-reflection aims at examining ourselves in light of God's Word and Spirit. David captured the concept best in the Psalms.

Q Read Psalm 139:23–24. Define self-reflection based on these verses.

If I had to name three areas for self-reflection, I would list actions, motives, and words. Do my actions align with God's words? Are my motives in sync with God's heart? Are my words reflective of a contrite heart?

Self-reflection is far from a form of navel gazing, a self-absorbed, inward look to see how we compare with others and to express how we feel about ourselves. Biblical self-reflection is "a humble, clear-minded assessment of ourselves through the gospel. It means looking to Scripture to see God's commands as the Holy Spirit points out the sins we harbor that are contrary to the Truth."[21]

When was the last time you took time and intentionally reflected on your actions, words, and motives in the light of God's Word?

The gift of the Lord's table is not just a celebration of what Christ did on the cross to purchase our freedom. It is also the gift of greater intimacy with the Lord through an invitation to deeper holiness. Each time we gather at the table with heads bowed and hearts examined, we're submitting to the belief that our joy depends on God and His ways. Do you believe that?

Let's Make This Personal

Take some time for self-reflection today. Use the self-reflection tool available in the resources section at the end of the book to see how you're doing in your walk with the Lord.

Today's Take Home Point

There is no place for sin in the
presence of a holy God.

Final Thought

How might God be inviting you to more regular times of confession, repentance, and biblical self-reflection?

Celebrate Good

As you consider our time in God's Word, write down one good thing you can celebrate in your life today.

Day 5: The Others

Reading: 1 Corinthians 11:17–34

Theme: The greatest test of your love for Jesus is how well you love others.

It's impossible to talk about the Lord's table without talking about "the others." God didn't set up the Communion table for each of His followers to partake of it at home on his or her own. While my introverted self might wish that I could isolate myself on an island for the rest of my life, Christ's plan for His people is not as individualistic as our American culture has trained us to be.

The fact of the Trinity should be a tip-off that we serve a God who loves community. He created us for fellowship with Himself but also with other people. He promised Abraham that he would have as many descendants as the stars in the sky! He referred to the church as the body of Christ—a body made up of many members. Whether you're fond of other Christians or not, the reality of the Lord's table is that it includes the others.

The problem is that "the others" can be challenging. While we might get along just fine with God, it's His people we struggle with. I wrote an entire book on the topic (*Fractured Faith: Finding Your Way Back to God in an Age of Deconstruction*). One of the biggest reasons that people stop going to church has nothing to do with God but everything to do with God's people.

The early church was no exception. The Christians in Corinth struggled with getting along with one another, and Paul had some instructions for them.

Read 1 Corinthians 11:17–22. What was the main problem the church of Corinth was dealing with?

The church was torn by dissension and divisions. People chose sides. They split into tribes. Remember high school? As painful as it was to encounter all the different factions in high school, at least graduation was only four years away! What was happening in the church at Corinth was shameful to the very name of Jesus. Even worse was that the behavior of the believers in Corinth perverted the Lord's Supper. What was intended as holy had become a sinful and selfish mockery of the name of Christ and an opportunity for the Corinthian believers to indulge themselves instead of honoring the Lord.

📍 Read verses 23 to 26. Why do you think Paul reminded them of the reason for the Lord's Supper after he rebuked them?

The people of Corinth needed perspective. They needed the gospel. Human conflict is prevalent everywhere we look, and especially in the church. It's not surprising that people fight—even in the church. It's how we overcome conflict that's the tricky part.

The greatest test of your love for Jesus is how well you love others.

Today, there are thousands of books and hours of webinars dedicated to conflict resolution. You could spend the rest of your life trying to implement strategies to resolve conflict. Paul's conflict-resolution method was radical: Go back to the cross. Embrace the gospel. Remember who you are and where you have come from.

📍 How does the gospel message free us to love others more freely?

⦿ Yesterday, we talked about self-reflection. One of the most important elements in self-reflection is humility. The Christians in Corinth had left humility by the wayside. They had adopted an attitude of pride and arrogance and were lording over one another. They needed biblical self-reflection. In the following verses, what does God teach us about how we are to think about ourselves and each other?

Romans 12:3

Galatians 6:3

Philippians 2:3–4

1 Corinthians 4:7

We need the gospel! Only Jesus can change us and create in us hearts that value others over ourselves. Only the example of Jesus, who humbled Himself and became obedient to His Father's will even to the point of death on the cross, will move us enough to humble ourselves for the sake of others. Paul finished his instructions to the church on this topic with one last point.

⦿ Read 1 Corinthians 11:33–34. What does it look like to wait for one another?

Have you ever run a race with someone who wasn't as fast as you, like a toddler? You know you could beat them, but you slow yourself down to run with them. Have you thought about why you do that? You do it because of love. It's love that moves us to wait for the others. It's love that convinces us to make space for the others. It's love that moved our Savior to pour out His blood to save us, the same love that now abides in us and is ready to change the world.

Do you ever wonder why the world is so slow to embrace Jesus? Perhaps they've been distracted by the way that Christians treat others. Perhaps it's time to change!

Let's Make This Personal

📍 Who are the others in your life who are hard to get along with? What are some practical ways you can practice "waiting for them"?

Today's Take Home Point

The most radical thing that will change the world is the kind of love that is possible only with Jesus.

Final Thought

How is God inviting you to celebrate His goodness through the practice of remembering what He has done for you?

Celebrate Good

As you consider our time in God's Word, write down one good thing you can celebrate in your life today.

Session 5: The Table of Remembrance

When I'm Apt to Forget

1 Corinthians 11:17-23; Matthew 26:20-28

Watch the session 5 video now. The video is available at DavidCCook.org/access, with access code TABLE.

1. When I am sinking in sin and in shame, I need to _____ the price that Jesus paid for my pardon.

2. When life is hard and victory seems impossible, I need to remember that Jesus has secured the victory for me through the power of the _____.

3. When I am lonely and longing for fellowship, I need to remember that _____ _____.

4. When I'm overwhelmed with suffering and am tired of waiting, I need to remember that deliverance _____.

Video Group Discussion Questions

After watching the video, discuss the following questions in your group.

📍 What is your biggest takeaway from this week's teaching?

📍 The picture of the bread and the wine is such a vivid reminder of what Jesus did for us on the cross. How does reflecting on Christ's sacrifice move you to want to change how you're living?

📍 Does the concept of holiness scare or excite you? How much of your holiness is your responsibility, and how much of it is God's?

📍 People can be hard to get along with. What are the biggest challenges you've faced in relating with other Christians?

📍 It is fitting to wrap up today's teaching with a communal meal of remembrance. Your leader will guide you in some quiet self-reflection, then lead you in celebrating the Lord's Supper together as you remember God's goodness to you through the gift of this table.

Week 5: The Table of Eternal Celebration—When Life Is Hard

Psalm 23:6
"Surely goodness and mercy shall follow me all the days of my life, and I shall dwell in the house of the LORD forever."

Introduction

Some meals are so awesome you never want to leave the table. Have you ever experienced that kind of meal? Perhaps your mind wanders back to your wedding day and the beautiful meal you shared with your beloved. Or maybe it was a dinner with friends where conversation flowed and the food was delicious.

I love few things more than a beautiful table set for a memorable meal. Though my cooking skills are limited, I follow enough lifestyle-food Instagram accounts to know exactly what perfection looks like. One of my dear friends, Rosa, is Italian. She is known to set some of the most beautiful tables. Everyone wants to be at Rosa's parties. You'll never go hungry at her house, and I've never had a meal at her table where conversation was lacking.

While the perfect meal might entail good food, the kind of meal most of us long for isn't just about the food. It's about the people. It's about an atmosphere of love and support and a meal that's not rushed—a meal without conflict. It's a meal that leaves us satisfied and wanting it to last forever.

The kind of meal most of us long for isn't just about the food. It's about the people.

Even if you've never experienced the kind of meal I'm describing, God has given each of us not only an internal sense that such a meal exists but also a longing for such a meal. I believe God gave us that internal knowledge so we will yearn for the most perfect meal, which He has prepared for those who love Him and call Him Lord. Perhaps this internal longing is what awakens us to our pursuit for more of God in our lives.

It's incredible to me that of all the places where God could have chosen to reveal His goodness to us, He often chose a table! That God feeds us is one of the most glorious mysteries in the world. We've already discussed how God created food for us to enjoy in the garden of Eden and how He later set a table for His people in the wilderness. Yet His proclivity to enjoy a meal with His people is tucked inside many other amazing stories in Scripture that we have yet to discuss.

Ever read Genesis 18, where Abraham was sitting in front of his tent when he was visited by three strangers? Abraham prepared a meal for them and later discovered that he was in fact feeding the Lord. In 1 Kings 19, the Lord found His servant Elijah in the bottomless pit of despair, and of all the things He could have done to encourage him, He made him a cake!

In the New Testament, we often get glimpses of Jesus sitting at a meal with His disciples and those who wanted to find out more about Him. One of my favorite meals recorded in the Gospels is the breakfast Jesus prepared for Peter in John 21 after Peter's epic failure. Jesus used breakfast to set the stage for healing Peter's heart. You know God is good if He uses food to heal us!

It shouldn't come as a surprise to us, then, that food will be part of our eternity. This week, we'll be spending our time studying the most awesome meal of them all: the marriage supper of the Lamb. Our Scripture reading will be in the book of Revelation, and I'm telling you, you're in for a treat—no pun intended!

You're going to find that the language in Revelation is water to the heart that is thirsty and hope for the one who is tired of waiting; it's healing for the hurting and pure joy for anyone who is ready for it. It's everything you hope it will be and more. I can't wait to dig into it with you!

Day 1: *Finally Here*

Reading: Revelation 19:1–10

Theme: A day is coming when everything will have been worth it.

Have you ever waited for something so long you could almost taste it? As kids, we used to wait with rabid anticipation for Christmas morning. Oh, we dreamed about it and imagined it, and then just when we thought it would never come, Christmas Eve gave way to Christmas morning. These days, most of us hold our breath until our vacation days, counting down the minutes and seconds until we can walk out the door to our desired destinations.

Trust me, I know all about waiting. I'm still waiting for my Prince Charming to come! There is something excruciatingly painful about waiting, and when the waiting finally ends, we hope that the outcome will be worth the wait.

We've been making our way through the Bible, stopping at some of the most memorable and important tables that God has set for us. We started our journey at the table of salvation. We saw how God used the blood of a perfect lamb to save His people and deliver them from Egypt. We then spent time at the table of unexpected belonging, where we came to understand more deeply how committed God is to His promises through the story of David and Mephibosheth.

Next was the site of the first miracle and the wedding meal at Cana, where we experienced God's overflowing abundance. And then last week, we sat at the table of remembrance, the Lord's table, and reviewed the goodness of God through the perfect sacrifice of Christ for our sins.

Your heart may already be full, but there's still one more table to come. This week's table is one that every Christian dreams of, even though most of us don't stop long enough to think about it. This week, we're going to focus on the table of eternal celebration, the marriage supper of the Lamb.

♀ Read Revelation 19:1–10. Describe, with as many details as you can, what the marriage supper of the Lamb will be like.

📍 What feelings go through your heart as you read the verses in this week's passage?

We're all waiting for something. We can taste it, even if we can barely describe it. In a culture of injustice, we're waiting for justice. In a world of evil, we're longing for good. In a life that is troubled, we're dreaming of a meal filled with joy instead of bickering. We're *longing* for something that we don't know quite how to define.

This longing plays out in many ways in our lives—mostly in frustration, and sometimes in anger. We jump from relationship to relationship, looking for fulfillment. We read books and donate money to worthy groups, hoping we can somehow fill the emptiness we're feeling. But the longing is still there.

C. S. Lewis said, "If we find ourselves with a desire that nothing in this world can satisfy, the most probable explanation is that we were made for another world."[22]

📍 What is it that you long for in your life? Try to put words to the feelings in your heart.

📍 Read Revelation 19:1–2 again. What do you learn in those verses about who God is?

Most of us forget how *just* our God is. In a world where evil seems to be winning and the powerful eat the weak, it's easy to assume that things will never change. Yet God's Word reminds us that justice is coming! God sees, He knows, and He will avenge His people someday!

How does the truth that God is just affect your outlook today? How might you live more boldly for Christ given the truth of who God is?

Focus on Revelation 19:6. What does it mean that God is omnipotent?

The word *omnipotent* can also mean "almighty." It is used nine times in the book of Revelation as a title for God.[23] The same God described in Revelation 19 is the God on the throne of the universe today. He's *your* King, if you've given your life to Jesus.

How does the reality of God's omnipotence change the way that you live your life today? What fears can be alleviated as you rest in God's omnipotence?

There is nothing God cannot do. To anyone discouraged that life is too hard, to anyone overwhelmed by the power of temptation in your life, to anyone who is tired of waiting, Revelation 19 is a reminder that things won't always be this way. A better day is coming.

This proclamation of justice and power is the kind of reminder that deserves a celebration!

📍 Read Revelation 19:7 again. What is the reason for rejoicing, according to John?

Revelation 19 is a reminder that things won't always be this way. A better day is coming.

After all the waiting, the feast of all feasts is finally here! We're going to focus on the bride and her groom tomorrow, but for today, let's end our time by rejoicing that no matter what we're going through right now, it won't be long before we'll be crying out with the saints and the angels: Hallelujah! For the Lord God Omnipotent reigns!

Are you ready for that day?

Let's Make This Personal

📍 Where in your life right now do you need the reminder of God's omnipotence and justice the most?

Today's Take Home Point

No matter how hard life is, we can hang on to the truth that someday all will be well.

Final Thought

♀ How is God using the coming celebration with Jesus to invite you to hold on to hope?

Celebrate Good

♀ As you consider our time in God's Word, write down one good thing you can celebrate in your life today.

Day 2: The Bride and the Groom

Reading: Revelation 19:1–10

Theme: The best human marriage serves as only a taste of all that still awaits us in Christ.

By God's design, every marriage requires both a bride and a groom. In the beginning, God created Adam and then gave him Eve. Though the gift of marriage was given by God for our enjoyment, God intended a deeper meaning for marriage. We talked about marriage earlier in this study, but today we're going to dig a little deeper into its symbolism.

Marriage is where we're all headed. Whether you're single or married, if you're a follower of Jesus, marriage is your destination. This magnificent final table called the marriage supper of the Lamb is not just a lofty idea for someone someday. It's *your* destiny, Christian! It's where anyone who has given his or her life to Jesus is headed. If you are a born-again follower of Jesus, washed by His blood and forgiven of your sins, you are part of the body of Christ—also known as the bride of Christ.

When it comes to the marriage supper of the Lamb, you're not just a spectator at a future event—you are actually *part* of the event.

As we've seen while we've been mapping the footsteps of God to us through His Word, there really is no greater celebratory table than this final one where we, the bride of Christ, will be united with Christ, our groom, forever.

◉ Let's start with Revelation 19:7–9. Describe the bride of Christ in your own words.

While we might assume that the clean and bright linen that clothed the bride is a picture of the imputed righteousness of Christ, Revelation 19:8 tells us that the meaning of the bride's attire actually points to the righteous acts of the saints, the practical results of righteousness in the believers' lives.[24]

◉ How might the meaning of the linen in verse 8 motivate you to live in greater obedience to Christ?

Several other important Scripture passages help us better understand the imagery of Christ as the groom and the church as the bride. It's worth studying a few of them here.

◉ Read Matthew 22:1–14. Without digging too deeply into the details of the parable, who is the king and who is the son in the story Jesus told?

◉ Read Matthew 25:1–13. In this parable, who is the bridegroom and who are the virgins?

◉ Read Ephesians 5:22–33. This is probably the most direct biblical teaching on the concept of Christ as the groom and the church as the bride. Write down the way the husband ought to treat his wife.

The more we meditate on what marriage ought to symbolize, the more we begin to understand the mind-boggling attack that's happening on marriage in our culture today. We have desecrated the meaning of marriage, loosened the covenant of marriage, skewed the roles in marriage, and disdained the very institution that ought to most closely represent the love of Christ for His bride, the church. Yet one day soon, you and I are going to witness the holiest marriage of all and celebrate our groom, Jesus, at the marriage supper of the Lamb.

♀ Can you think of some ways Satan has attempted to destroy the truth about marriage? What are some of the ways our culture's perspective on marriage has affected your perception of marriage?

Marriage takes work and intentionality. It takes devotion, and devotion takes patience and forbearance. In our broken world, it's easy to get distracted from the things that matter the most. In fact, Paul warned us about it.

♀ Read 2 Corinthians 11:1–3. What are some of the ways Satan might be leading you astray from a sincere and pure devotion to Christ?

Fortunately for us, we have a groom who never quits being faithful to us. He knows our propensity to wander from Him, yet He is committed to us forever.

The best human marriage serves as only a taste of all that still awaits us in Christ.

There is probably no greater encouragement for the Christian who is prone to wander from God (and that's all of us) than the book of Hosea. God used Hosea the prophet to show the people of Israel just how faithful and good He is to His children. He asked Hosea to marry a prostitute, Gomer, knowing she would abandon her marriage vows. God then told Hosea to seek Gomer and bring her back to him even when she didn't deserve it.

The whole point of the marriage of Hosea was to teach us just how deep God's love and His faithfulness for us is, always pursuing us even when we willfully sin against Him. The goal of the Christian life, though, and the goal of studying the Bible is to experience God's love for us so deeply that we will be less prone to wander from Him.

Q What are some specific ways that you have experienced God's love in your life?

In Revelation 19:9, John wrote, "Blessed are those who are invited to the marriage supper of the Lamb." There is no more important question than this: Will you be at the marriage supper of the Lamb?

Let's Make This Personal

Q When you consider that Christ is the groom and you are part of the bride of Christ, how would you describe your relationship with Him right now? What needs to change in order for you to know your groom more intimately?

Today's Take Home Point

> While human marriage might bring temporary happiness, it is spiritual marriage to the Lamb of God that brings everlasting security and joy.

Final Thought

How might God be inviting you to deeper satisfaction in Him, no matter your marital status?

Celebrate Good

As you consider our time in God's Word, write down one good thing you can celebrate in your life today.

Day 3: Christ Our Groom

Reading: Revelation 19:11–16

Theme: Eternity will only begin to unveil the beauty and magnificence of Jesus.

I have another confession to make. It's a little embarrassing, but here goes: I am a hopeless romantic. Though I've been engaged twice and have adopted a cynical persona, you don't need to dig too deeply to find out that I love a good love story.

Hallmark movies? Sign me up, though I'll never admit it in public. Romantic comedies? I've seen them all. I especially love the stories where the guy rescues the girl and they live happily ever after. I know it sounds hokey and old-fashioned and is an affront to most feminists, but it's true. I'm hoping we're too far into this study for you to bail on me, so stick with me a bit longer.

Whether you are into romantic movies or not, I think most of us would agree that what makes a story good is the strength of its characters. And there is no greater hero than the one who willingly sacrifices himself for the sake of his bride.

We're going to spend our time today focused on the groom. I hope that throughout this study, your understanding of who Jesus is has grown, as has your love for Him. And yet there is more! Even the most seasoned follower of Jesus has barely scratched the surface of the goodness of Christ. Oh, to think that we will someday see Him more clearly! I can't wait until that day. Our text today gives us a taste of what's to come.

Read Revelation 19:11–16. Write down as many things about Jesus as you can identify in this passage.

Which of the descriptions of Jesus touches you most deeply? Why do you think it resonates with you?

There are so many amazing ways to describe Christ, but few capture His essence like the words in Revelation 19:11, where He "is called Faithful and True."

ⵔ What do these words mean? Try to define them here.

ⵔ In what ways has Christ most obviously demonstrated His faithfulness to you?

The book of Revelation was written by the beloved disciple, John, while he was exiled on the isle of Patmos. What was meant for evil—his imprisonment in exile—became the very tool that God used to get John's attention and to inspire him through the Holy Spirit to write the letter that tells us about the end of time and our eternal future as believers. If anyone could use a reminder of God's eternal faithfulness to His children, it was poor, exiled John!

ⵔ How might the picture of the marriage supper of the Lamb have reinforced John's belief in the faithfulness of Christ?

I need regular reminders of God's faithfulness to me. Too often in my life, I become so focused on my own problems that I forget God's faithfulness. His faithfulness becomes an academic term used simply to describe who God is. Yet it is in meditating deeply on the Word of God that our perspective shifts from one of sorrow to joy. At the Lord's table, we remember what Christ has already done for us. In the pages of Revelation, we rehearse the future that God has promised us, and we are able to hang on to joy no matter our present circumstances.

Eternity will only begin to unveil the beauty and magnificence of Jesus.

Everything in this world is fleeting. I get so caught up thinking that my joy hinges on God providing the things I think I need to be happy—a husband, a legacy, a secure IRA account. I get so caught up in my earthly circumstances that I become of no use to the heavenly kingdom. But while earthly provisions and answers to prayers might give me temporary joy, it's the truth about God's faithfulness that pivots me to true joy.

📍 On a scale of one to ten, how would you describe your joy meter? What stands in the way of your joy?

Jesus is committed to your joy. He gave His life for your joy. He is clothed with a robe dipped in blood for your sake. His name is the Word of God, and His sword is ready to be wielded against the attack of the enemy. He is your groom who is preparing a home for you in heaven right now!

📍 Read Revelation 19:15–16. Write down the words that express Christ's power.

How does the picture of God ruling over everything give you courage no matter what you're facing in this season?

While the troubles of this earth can feel eternal, it is by focusing on the Word of God that our vision is recalibrated. Ours is a love story that no power in hell and no force on earth can destroy. No wonder Paul prays that we, "being rooted and grounded in love, may have strength to comprehend with all the saints what is the breadth and length and height and depth, and to know the love of Christ that surpasses knowledge" (Eph. 3:17–19).

Do you know His love? Are you anticipating this marriage supper of the Lamb? Now tell me you're not a hopeless romantic too!

Let's Make This Personal

One of the best ways to assess how truly you believe in God's love for you is to gauge your level of joy. What does your joy meter say about your belief in God's love, faithfulness, and goodness?

Today's Take Home Point

Nothing will alleviate your cares more than picturing Christ on a white horse fighting for you!

Final Thought

📍 When you picture Christ on a white horse fighting for you, do any thoughts occur to you about how God might be inviting you to deeper joy?

Celebrate Good

📍 As you consider our time in God's Word, write down one good thing you can celebrate in your life today.

Day 4: We Win!
Reading: Revelation 19:17–21
Theme: A day is coming when evil will be destroyed forever.

When it comes to your eternal soul, existence is not meant to stay hard forever. In fact, the very opposite is true for the follower of Jesus. One day soon, we will be feasting at the best table yet—the great marriage supper of the Lamb. What a meal this will be!

Maybe you're not into romantic comedies. Maybe you're not a hopeless romantic. If you're into action and adventure movies, today's Scripture passage is for you. If you're one to relish victories, you're in for a treat. Everyone knows that every great feast has multiple courses, and today's course is victory.

⚲ Read Revelation 19:17–21. Describe what happens to God's enemies here.

⚲ Read Revelation 20:1–3. While we, the bride of Christ, will be celebrating at the marriage supper of the Lamb, what will happen to the devil?

Do you wonder if evil will ever be defeated? Do you long for temptations to stop? Do you look around you and see the darkness in our world getting darker? Do you ask yourself where God is? Don't you worry. There is coming a day when Satan will be defeated forever.

The book of Revelation reveals ample details about the future doom of Satan, but we don't have to wait until eternity to experience victory against the evil one. Let's spend a few moments reviewing some Scriptures on victory.

Read Colossians 2:15. What did Christ accomplish at the cross?

Read 1 Corinthians 15:55–57. What kind of power does sin have over the follower of Jesus?

Read Matthew 28:18. Who has authority over everything?

Read Hebrews 2:8. What is under the control of Jesus?

Do you ever wonder why, if Satan is already defeated, God doesn't simply obliterate him now? Why has God given him a window of time to go on wreaking havoc on humanity?

Take some time and think about possible reasons why evil continues even though Christ has already triumphed over evil at the cross.

While we might not fully understand God's reasons for delaying the eternal defeat of Satan, perhaps there is no greater reason than the glory of God. John Piper wrote:

> There is more glory that will come to Jesus Christ by our sharing in the suffering of Christ and holding on to his supreme value than if we had been able to say "Satan, depart!" and never have another problem. And I think the reason for that is the glory of God shines most brightly, when we are seen to be supremely satisfied in Christ in spite of Satan's torments—which exist—rather than having those torments removed and liking Jesus because of it. It is when you love Jesus in spite of it and through it that his glory shines most brightly, rather than when we have life made easier for us by its removal, and we like Jesus because of it.[25]

The glory of God shines most brightly when we are seen to be supremely satisfied in Christ in spite of Satan's torments. It is when you love Jesus in spite of it and through it that His glory shines most brightly. While the idea of someday being delivered from evil forever should bring us great joy, I wonder if our resting in the protection of our Savior right now is what brings *Christ* great joy. Are you willing to risk it? Are you willing to fight for joy even though your circumstances may not change right away?

The glory of God shines most brightly when we are seen to be supremely satisfied in Christ in spite of Satan's torments.

Let's Make This Personal

📍 How does knowing that Satan is already defeated change the way you view temptation in your life right now?

Today's Take Home Point

Though complete victory over evil is still yet
to come, victory is ours in Christ right now.

Final Thought

📍 If you were to weigh your earthly struggles against God's authority over all, what might you conclude about how God is inviting you to victory right now?

Celebrate Good

📍 As you consider our time in God's Word, write down one good thing you can celebrate in your life today.

Day 5: Happily Ever After

Reading: Revelation 22:1–17

Theme: The goodness of God is experienced in His promise of our happily-ever-after.

I already confessed to being a hopeless romantic, so it should come as no surprise to you that I'm also a sucker for happily-ever-afters.

We've spent the last six weeks feasting together on the goodness of God. In the middle of life's wilderness seasons, we've been offered the gift of God's goodness at five different tables—the table of salvation, the table of unexpected belonging, the table of overflowing satisfaction, the table of remembrance, and finally this week at the table of eternal celebration.

We have been given so many reasons to celebrate. We have feasted on the coming marriage supper of the Lamb and the beauty of our groom, Jesus. We've been assured of the destruction of our enemy and the promise of living eternally with our conquering Lord. We've been reminded that as beautiful as our future is, we've already been given a guarantee of God's presence and victory over evil right here and right now!

We don't have to wait to taste the goodness of God. We don't have to wait to experience intimacy with Christ. Someday, our union will be complete, but until then, we have the promise of Christ living in us and the Spirit with us (Eph. 1:13–14). While so much of what we long for in Jesus is yet to come, we've also been given everything we need in Him right now (2 Pet. 1:3). And yet there is something powerful that stems from reaching toward all that is yet to come.

Today's Scripture reading will focus on our happily-ever-after. Someday, all our tears will be dried and the totality of our worries will be abolished. Someday, the very things that you and I are losing sleep over won't even be a distant memory. Let's take some time and dream about that day.

♦ Read Revelation 22:1–17. The text is longer than our usual reading, but it's so rich to study. Write down the emotions you feel as you read this passage.

I mentioned earlier that the Christian walk is not simply agreement with a creed or an intellectual assent to a set of beliefs. While it is important to have a solid understanding of God's Word and His ways, the Christian life is also a sensory experience. It is a relationship with God through His Son, Jesus, that ultimately satisfies our hunger.

The more I think about why God created food for us to enjoy, the more I am convinced that He uses hunger to point us to a deeper spiritual longing for Him. What we eat ultimately fills us and transforms us. As a steady diet of junk food eventually will take a toll on your body, so filling your soul with anything but God's Word will leave you feeling sick and lethargic. Let's take time instead to feast on God's Word and experience a heart of fullness and satisfaction.

📍 Focus on Revelation 22:17. What is the invitation God offers us?

📍 Where in your life is God inviting you to become more satisfied in Him?

We tend to think that our problems are material. If we only had more money, we would become more satisfied. Or we think of our problems as sexual. If only we were married and had a healthy sex life with our marriage partner, we would be more satisfied. We think our problem is not bearing enough fruit. If only we bore more fruit for the kingdom of God, we would be satisfied. Or we think our problems are physical. If only we were thinner or prettier, we would be more satisfied.

Yet God invites us to satisfaction without reference to any of those things. His solution for our joy and satisfaction is *Himself.* And the way to this satisfaction is simply to come to Him for it!

📍 What has kept you from coming to God in the areas where you're hurting the most?

You don't need to hurt anymore. You don't need to wait for anything to change in your life in order to experience more joy. God's goodness is that He's made Himself fully available to you right now. Jesus is coming again, and soon. But until He does, you've been invited to feast with Him at the table He's set for you wherever you find yourself right now, even in your wilderness places.

Have you eaten at the table of His salvation? Rejoice in the rescue you've been given. Have you been invited to a table you don't feel you deserve? You're right. Though undeserved, the invitation is still offered to you! Do you long for the filling of your empty spaces? God invites you to the table of abundant satisfaction. Are you apt to forget? Don't worry. You've been gifted the table of remembrance. Take the bread, drink the wine, and remember His goodness to you. Do you long for your happily-ever-after? Don't worry. It's coming. Your groom awaits you at the marriage feast of the Lamb!

> ## You don't need to hurt anymore. God's goodness is that He's made Himself fully available to you right now.

You don't have to be sad anymore. You don't have to be afraid. You don't have to wonder where God is. He's with you. He's for you. He's made a place at the table for you, and He's waiting for you with a smile on His face. You are loved. You belong. You're a child of the King!

As we conclude this Bible study series, let's take some time and reflect on all we've learned.

Let's Make This Personal

 What are the two or three biggest lessons you've learned about God's goodness in this Bible study? What are some of the specific ways God has revealed His goodness to you at the table? Where in your life do you still long to change?

Today's Take Home Point

> If you walk under the authority of Christ, you can rest assured that your story with God ends in a happily-ever-after.

Final Thought

 What is God's invitation to you as you conclude this Bible study series?

Celebrate Good

 As you consider our time in God's Word, write down one good thing you can celebrate in your life today.

Session 6: The Table of Eternal Celebration

When Life Is Hard

Revelation 19:6–21

Watch the session 6 video now. The video is available at DavidCCook.org/access, with access code TABLE.

1. There is coming a day when all I've hoped for and have been promised will _____ _____.

2. There is coming a day when all my tears will turn to _____.

3. A day is coming when my _____ with Christ will be even more complete.

4. There is coming a day when the evil one will be _____ forever.

5. There is coming a day when all my hunger will be _____ forever.

Video Group Discussion Questions

After watching the video, discuss the following questions in your group.

- What are you most looking forward to at the marriage supper of the Lamb?

- Though Satan will be utterly defeated someday, you've been given victory over him right now. How does knowing that you have power over sin and evil change the way you view your struggle with sin? Why is this easier said than done?

- What are some of the practices that you've established (or plan to establish) to experience God's goodness in your life?

- You can tell what satisfies you by where you turn to when you're tired and hurting. What do the places you turn to say about your belief in the ability of God to satisfy you?

- What you eat transforms you. How has the time spent feasting on God's Word changed you in the last six weeks?

Final Thought

Well, we made it! It's been so great to spend the last six weeks with you. I hope you have found yourself drawn closer to the Lord. I trust that your faith roots are deeper than they were when we started. And although we've never met, I feel like we're already friends.

As your friend, I would love to stay in touch with you. There are a number of ways for us to connect:

1. Social media: Follow me on social media platforms @linaabujamra.
2. Check out more Bible study resources at www.livingwithpower.org.
3. Send me an email and tell me how God has used this study in your life: lina@livingwithpower.org.

Let's stay in touch—but more importantly, let's stay close to Jesus. Without Him, no human feast will truly satisfy!

I love you guys.

Lina

Video Access QR Code

Six-Session Video Series

Leader's Guide

Thank you for leading a group through this Bible study. I am grateful for your willingness to share yourself and help others dig deeper into God's Word. I hope this leader's guide will help you as you study Scripture together.

The basic outline of each group session will be:

1. Discuss your personal study time from the past week. This leader's guide will point you to specific questions from the week to reflect on and answer with your group. The questions in the leader's guide are just a guide. You don't have to use all of the questions each week. Use them as a springboard for discussing what God has done in your group members' hearts that week.

2. Watch the video and take notes on what you hear.

3. Discuss the group questions on the Video Group Discussion Questions page.

4. Pray and dismiss.

Ideally, you will need to schedule an hour each week for a study like this one in order to have time for both group discussion and watching the video teaching.

Tips on Leading

1. Pray. Nothing will move the hearts of the men and women in your group like prayer will. Set aside time each week to pray for everyone in your group. Get to know them and bring their needs before the Lord regularly.

2. Guide. Your job isn't to change the people in your group, but to help guide them. Listen carefully to what everyone shares. Be willing to be vulnerable, and you'll set the tone for your group to do the same. Lead by example. Be consistent and trustworthy.

3. Connect. Be creative during the week to connect with your group. Use social media as well as texts and email to encourage the members of your group, share prayer requests, and connect with them.

Session 1: Introduction

Use this first session to begin to build relationships with your group. Familiarize them with the content of the study. Preview the study with the members of your group so they know what's coming.

1. Be sure each member in your group has a copy of *A Table in the Wilderness*.

2. Invite each member of your group to introduce themselves and tell something about themselves.

3. Ask what drew each member to the study.

4. Ask the group to share what they already know about God feeding His people throughout the Scriptures and if they've ever thought about why He has chosen the table as a place to reveal His goodness.

5. Ask each person to share what they hope to learn in this study.

6. Before you begin the video, ask each person to silently think about where they need to experience God's goodness in their life right now. Have them write down their thoughts in the space provided or a separate notebook, or on a device.

7. Watch the introduction video and answer the discussion questions in the Video Group Discussion Questions section.

8. Instruct the members of your group to complete the week 1 homework section in the study guide and come ready to discuss it next week.

9. Pray and dismiss.

Session 2: The Table of Salvation

1. Questions to ask your group:

a. Read Exodus 12:1–14 together. Does it surprise you that God planned a meal to save His people from Egypt?

b. Where in your life do you need rescuing right now? How does the story of God rescuing the people of Israel encourage you to keep on waiting?

c. What part of the Passover meal moved you the most, especially as you consider the symbolic practices that were meant to point to the coming Messiah?

d. What is your response to the fairness of God in saving only those families whose doors were covered with the blood of a lamb?

e. Was there a verse from your reading and study this week that impacted you the most? Which was it, and how did it impact you?

f. We spent some time this week talking about what it means to have a hard heart versus a soft heart. How would you describe your heart toward God in this season of your life?

2. Watch video session 2 and discuss the questions in the Video Group Discussion Questions section.

3. Pray and dismiss.

Session 3: The Table of Unexpected Belonging

1. Questions to ask your group:

a. Read 2 Samuel 9 together. Let's take some time and discuss your reactions to the story of David and Mephibosheth. What did you love about it?

b. David's example of kindness sticks out in a world that's not kind. Why is it so hard to be kind these days? What practical ways can you resolve to be kind to others, especially those who don't deserve it?

c. Put yourself in Mephibosheth's shoes and think about David as a picture of Jesus. How does the story affect you at a deeper level with this in mind?

d. That Mephibosheth was crippled is not accidental. We all have areas in our lives that we feel make us less deserving and cause us to hide. Are you comfortable talking about some of those areas in your life and how God has helped you find freedom to live without shame?

e. What keeps you from showing up regularly at the table of God's abundant grace? What might someone miss out on who refuses to receive God's grace?

2. Watch video session 3 and discuss the questions in the Video Group Discussion Questions section.

3. Pray and dismiss.

Session 4: The Table of Overflowing Satisfaction

1. Questions to ask your group:

a. Read John 2:1–11 together. What do you love most about this story and the fact that Jesus used the wedding as the scene for His first miracle?

b. Did Jesus' reaction to Mary initially surprise you? How were you encouraged by Mary's response to Jesus?

c. What are some of the empty spaces in your life that you're longing for God to fill?

d. The entire scene at the wedding of Cana screams of joy and utter delight. Does your Christian life reflect this delight, or do you tend to be a cup-half-empty Christian? In what practical ways can you change as you learn to delight in Christ?

e. Obedience is the key to breakthrough. Where in your life do you need to obey Christ more completely?

f. Real breakthrough happens when you believe the goodness of God no matter the outcome. What are some ways you are learning to live so that joy doesn't hinge on getting the outcome you want but it hinges on the person of Christ in your life?

2. Watch video session 4 and discuss the questions in the Video Group Discussion Questions section.

3. Pray and dismiss.

Session 5: The Table of Remembrance

1. Questions to ask your group:

a. Read 1 Corinthians 11:17–34 together. Talk about your experience with the Lord's Supper. Have you ever participated in the Lord's Supper? Do you approach it with seriousness? Why?

b. What are some of the things about the gospel that you are prone to forget in your daily living?

c. How does forgetting gospel truth influence your attitudes and reactions? What are some common emotions you're living with that wouldn't stand a chance against the truth of the gospel?

d. While physical bread satisfies your body, it's the Lord Jesus who alone is able to satisfy you completely. Have you found Jesus to be completely satisfying in your life? Why, or why not?

e. Community is a big part of the Lord's table and the Christian life in general. What has your experience with Christian community been?

2. Watch video session 5 and discuss the questions in the Video Group Discussion Questions section.

3. Pray and dismiss.

Session 6: The Table of Eternal Celebration

This is the last week together with your group. Congratulate the people in your group for finishing strong. Share highs and lows. Take time to celebrate the wins. Challenge the members of your group to continue to study God's Word and to share what they've learned with the people in their lives.

1. Questions to ask your group:

   a. What stuck out the most for you in this week's study? It may be a verse or a sentence or a thought or idea.

   b. Read Revelation 19:6–21 together. What brings you deep joy as you read this text of Scripture out loud? What are you most looking forward to in that marriage supper of the Lamb?

   c. When you consider God's power and justice, how are you motivated to live with less fear and more boldness?

   d. Are you living as if Jesus is indeed the victorious King of your life? What areas in your life can change now that you're picturing Jesus as victorious ruler of all?

   e. On a scale of one to ten, where would the needle of your joy meter be pointing right now?

   f. Where in your life do you long to experience more of God's satisfying joy?

2. Watch video session 6 and discuss the questions in the Video Group Discussion Questions section.

3. Pray and dismiss.

Spiritual Exercises

One of the main goals of Bible study is to encounter God more deeply. While learning about God through the study of Scripture will enlarge our minds to worship God more purely, spending time meditating on Scripture will fuel our hearts to experience God more intimately.

To that end, I've compiled a spiritual exercise in the *lectio divina* style to help you meditate more deeply on God. It's designed to be read at the end of each week's homework.

Lectio divina is a contemplative way to read the Bible. It dates back to the early centuries of the Christian church and was established as a monastic practice by Benedict in the sixth century. It is a way of praying the Scriptures that leads us deeper into God's Word.

Lectio divina helps us slow down. In it, we read a short Bible passage more than once. As we chew on it slowly and carefully, the Scripture begins to speak to us in a fresh way. Lectio is a practice that considers Scripture as a meeting place for a personal encounter with the living God. In some ways, it can be described as more *hearty* than *heady*. Through it, we allow ourselves to be formed in the likeness of Christ. It is about formation rather than instruction.

We will follow the same pattern for each week's reading. It starts with silence. A good approach to meditating on the Scriptures follows this template:

On your first reading of the passage: Listen.

As you read the passage, listen for a word or phrase that attracts you. Allow it to arise from the passage as if it is God's word for you today.

Second reading of the passage: Ponder.

As you read the passage again, ask how this word or phrase speaks to your life and why it has connected with you. Ponder it carefully. Sit in silence, and then frame a single sentence that begins to say aloud what this word or phrase is speaking to you.

Third reading of the passage: Pray.

As you read the passage for the last time, ask what Christ is calling out from you. What is it that you need to do or relinquish or take on as a result of what God is saying to you in this word or phrase? In the silence that follows the reading, pray for the grace of the Spirit to plant this word in your heart.

Spiritual Exercise Week 1

Getting Out of Egypt

Exodus 12:21–28

Then Moses called all the elders of Israel and said to them, "Go and select lambs for yourselves according to your clans, and kill the Passover lamb. Take a bunch of hyssop and dip it in the blood that is in the basin, and touch the lintel and the two doorposts with the blood that is in the basin. None of you shall go out of the door of his house until the morning. For the LORD will pass through to strike the Egyptians, and when he sees the blood on the lintel and on the two doorposts, the LORD will pass over the door and will not allow the destroyer to enter your houses to strike you. You shall observe this rite as a statute for you and for your sons forever. And when you come to the land that the LORD will give you, as he has promised, you shall keep this service. And when your children say to you, 'What do you mean by this service?' you shall say, 'It is the sacrifice of the LORD's Passover, for he passed over the houses of the people of Israel in Egypt, when he struck the Egyptians but spared our houses.'" And the people bowed their heads and worshiped.

Then the people of Israel went and did so; as the LORD had commanded Moses and Aaron, so they did.

Read the passage out loud once.

Now close your eyes and take a few deep breaths. Pray with me: "O God, I pray that You will help me to hear You speak during this time of meditation on Your Word. I open my hands to You. I open my ears to You."

Pause ten seconds.

Imagine that you are standing among the Israelites that day. It's hot under the Egyptian sun, but you hardly notice. Your life has been turned upside down the last few weeks. You try to remember the events that led up to this unexpected moment. It feels like not that long ago you were hauling bricks on your back under the watchful gaze of your slave master, praying that you'd stay unnoticed. You'd seen enough of your friends beaten and tortured. You catch visions of huddling with your family at night, praying for deliverance but convinced that God had forgotten you and your people.

Then your mind wanders back to that crazy day when Moses showed up. Hardly anyone believed that God had sent him. In fact, most people didn't even remember Moses from forty years earlier. But you did. You remembered the story of him murdering an Egyptian and running for his life.

News of his return rocked you to the core. You could hardly believe the boldness Moses carried. Like a man on a mission, he showed up—unafraid. Like a man backed by a mighty God, Moses took on Pharaoh. For the first time in a long time, hope crept slowly into your heart. You find yourself smirking now as you think back to what happened next. The plagues. Even now, your jaw goes slack as you review the show your God put on to free you all from Pharaoh.

Someone accidentally bumps into you, bringing you back to the present. The people's mumbling grows louder. What is Moses saying? He wants us to … what? Find a lamb, an unblemished lamb, and kill it? Where does he think someone like you can find a lamb? How in the world will everyone find a lamb? But also, you've never killed a lamb before. What if you're too scared to do it? How serious is Moses about this plan?

You weigh your options. On one hand, you could ignore Moses. You could just hope for the best. But on the other hand, what if Moses is right? What if God is serious about this plan?

You get a feeling that your life is about to really change. One thing you're sure of, you can't go on living like usual. You wish you could ask God some questions.

♀ What questions do you have for God?

Read the passage again.
Pause for ten seconds.

You listen again. This time you hear it more clearly. It seems that God's plan is not to leave you in Egypt. It seems as if God is inviting you into a new adventure. It seems as if everything you've ever prayed for is on the verge of happening. It's hot and you're thirsty. You're not 100 percent sure which direction to go. You say a silent prayer and ponder what to do.

♀ What are your fears? What are your hopes? Where is God in your imagination now? What questions do you hear others asking? Here's a better question: What do you have to lose if you just do what God is asking?

Pause ten seconds.

♀ Now close your eyes and take a few deep breaths. In what area in your life do you have questions about God's plans? Where in your life is God giving you the invitation to risk believing in Him for more? If you're unsure of what next step to take, spend some time jotting down what you know God is asking you to do, as crazy as it may seem. Why are you so afraid of stepping into His way?

📍 Ask yourself honestly how faithful you have been in carrying out the steps you know God has already asked you to take. How can you stifle your fear of the impossible and simply take a step of faith toward God?

What if your entire future rested on what you did today? What if your freedom hinged on your next step of obedience? Are you willing to risk discomfort in order to lean into joy?

Spiritual Exercise Week 2

Come Alive

2 Samuel 9:3–8

And the king said, "Is there not still someone of the house of Saul, that I may show the kindness of God to him?" Ziba said to the king, "There is still a son of Jonathan; he is crippled in his feet." The king said to him, "Where is he?" And Ziba said to the king, "He is in the house of Machir the son of Ammiel, at Lo-debar." Then King David sent and brought him from the house of Machir the son of Ammiel, at Lo-debar. And Mephibosheth the son of Jonathan, son of Saul, came to David and fell on his face and paid homage. And David said, "Mephibosheth!" And he answered, "Behold, I am your servant." And David said to him, "Do not fear, for I will show you kindness for the sake of your father Jonathan, and I will restore to you all the land of Saul your father, and you shall eat at my table always." And he paid homage and said, "What is your servant, that you should show regard for a dead dog such as I?"

Read the passage out loud once.

Now close your eyes and take a few deep breaths. Pray with me: "O God, I pray that You will help me to hear You speak during this time of meditation on Your Word. I open my hands to You. I open my ears to You."

Pause for ten seconds.

Imagine you're Mephibosheth. Your heart is beating faster than you've ever felt it beat before. You're sure everyone sees it. Your feet are sore. You've just spent two whole days traveling to the palace. Up until a few days ago, you thought you were safe. You thought no one would find you. You never expected to be called to the presence of the king.

You try to remember your father, Jonathan. You'd heard that he and King David were great friends, but you hardly believed it. Your only memory of those days was that one fateful night. Even that night remains fuzzy in your mind, but you do remember the pain. You've been told the story enough times by now to know every detail by heart. Your nanny, in a frenzy to escape, grabbed you and ran. She was almost out of danger when she tripped. You fell. The rest, as they say, is history. Today, you've got a limp to show for her love and fear. You're crippled. Everyone knows you as a cripple. Thankfully, until today, only a few people paid attention to you.

Two days ago, your life changed. What had been a miserable but steady existence was shaken to the core. You received the message through Ziba, your father's servant who had pity enough to care for you. He told you that Kind David was looking for you.

You'd spent two sleepless nights tossing and turning. Surely David's plan is to kill you. How could anyone believe that David intended to help you? Why would he do that? Even a crippled man isn't naive enough to buy that line! But what choice do you have? When the king calls, the people answer. How could a dead dog like you do otherwise?

Yet here you are, your heart beating madly. You can hardly believe your ears. Did King David really just say what you thought he said?

📍 What comes to your mind as you stand before the king and listen to him speak?

📍 What are you afraid of? What do you secretly hope for?

Read the passage again.
Pause for ten seconds.

Now listen closely. Lean in a little more. David is speaking, but you're too shaken to understand his words. Ziba nudges you in the side. You almost tip over. You feel you're living in a dream. You try to mouth an answer to the king, but your words come out in a mumble.

You're so upset with yourself. What if David changes his mind? What if you ruin your chance of saying yes? You lean in and try again. You feel wetness on your cheeks and realize you're crying. Pretty soon, everyone around you is tearing up too. You might have also heard Ziba shout in joy. The whole thing seems too good to be true. *Why? Why would David extend this kindness to a dead dog like me?*

◉ Describe the scene. Why is everybody so moved? What are you most happy about? What do you wish you could express to King David?

Pause for ten seconds.

Is that a smile on your face? Now think about God for a moment. Think about the last few years in your life. What were the things you prayed about leading up to today? Think about the shame of your physical disability. Why did you spend all these years in hiding? What were you afraid others would find out about you? Remember how scared you've been that the king would someday find you? Now that you've gotten to know the king a little, are you still just as afraid of him? How has your relationship with the king already changed? What would you like to thank God for?

You look around at all the people in the palace. Never in your life did you imagine life could be so good.

You say thank you to the king. Over and over again, your lips move of their own accord saying thank you, thank you, thank you.

Pause for ten seconds.

◉ Can you feel the joy? Can you see the miracle that the kindness of the king has unleashed? Can you feel the healing taking shape in your heart? In what ways have you already been freed from your own prison of shame?

You know that tomorrow you'll be expected to show up at the table of the king for a meal. For a second, you feel the shame creep in. *What will they say? What if they hate me enough to want to hurt me? What if they laugh at me because of my limp?* Are you willing to ignore what other people will think of you and focus on the king? Are you willing to risk limping your way to the table in order to feast with the king?

You smile to yourself. The dead dog has been brought back to life, and ain't nobody gonna stand in your way.

Are you willing to ignore what other people will think of you and focus on the king?

Spiritual Exercise Week 3

What If ...

John 2:1–11

On the third day there was a wedding at Cana in Galilee, and the mother of Jesus was there. Jesus also was invited to the wedding with his disciples. When the wine ran out, the mother of Jesus said to him, "They have no wine." And Jesus said to her, "Woman, what does this have to do with me? My hour has not yet come." His mother said to the servants, "Do whatever he tells you."

Now there were six stone water jars there for the Jewish rites of purification, each holding twenty or thirty gallons. Jesus said to the servants, "Fill the jars with water." And they filled them up to the brim. And he said to them, "Now draw some out and take it to the master of the feast." So they took it. When the master of the feast tasted the water now become wine, and did not know where it came from (though the servants who had drawn the water knew), the master of the feast called the bridegroom and said to him, "Everyone serves the good wine first, and when people have drunk freely, then the poor wine. But you have kept the good wine until now." This, the first of his signs, Jesus did at Cana in Galilee, and manifested his glory. And his disciples believed in him.

Read the passage out loud once.

Now close your eyes and take a few deep breaths. Pray with me: "O God, I pray that You will help me to hear You speak during this time of meditation on Your Word. I open my hands to You. I open my ears to You."

Pause for ten seconds.

Imagine you're a servant at the wedding. You're watching a debacle unfold. What started as a joyous occasion is about to hit some turbulence. Your friend Suha just told you that the wine has run out. You run to the wine jars to double-check, and you can hardly believe it. How did this happen? Such a disaster is unheard of at a wedding. You brace yourself for the anger of the master of the feast.

Then you notice Mary quietly approach her son Jesus. You've met Jesus before in town. He's a fixture in Nazareth, the polite son of Mary and Joseph. You've heard of His solid work as a carpenter. You're surprised to hear Mary tell Jesus that the wine has run out. What does she expect Jesus the carpenter to do about it? At first, Jesus looks like He's got nothing to offer, but then you notice Mary making her way to where you stand with the servants. She looks you directly in the eye and tells you to do whatever Jesus instructs.

What? Why does she expect us to do what Jesus tells us to do? We don't work for Jesus. You're puzzled and intrigued. You've always loved drama and can't wait to see what will happen.

You look up and notice Jesus walking toward you. Something about the way He's walking catches your attention. It's like He's walking with purpose. It's like He knows what's about to happen. By this point, the wine is completely out, and the guests are starting to mumble, but Jesus doesn't seem fazed by any of it.

He's quiet for a moment. He's deliberate, at peace. Then He looks you in the eyes and speaks: "Fill the jars with water."

You can't help but laugh out loud. You think He's lost his mind. There are more than a few jars. Where does He think we will come up with the water? And what does He think we will do with the water? Serve it out and tell everyone it is wine?

You look sideways and catch your friend's eye with the obvious questions: What are we supposed to do? Is this guy for real, or has He lost His mind?

Read the passage again.
Pause for ten seconds.

What goes through your mind as you consider the cost of doing what Jesus has asked? You realize that you could just walk away. It's not your wedding, after all. You're just a servant here. You don't care about the wine at all. But a part of you is dying to know what He's got in mind. A part of you is riveted by the man who has asked you to do the ridiculous.

What is it about Jesus that has caused you to pause? What do you hope will happen in the story?

You make up your mind: you're going to see it through. You start hustling to the place where the water is kept, and you notice that the other servants are hustling too. There's an excitement in the air, even in the face of the unknown. What could happen if you did exactly what Jesus asked? What if a miracle were to take place? What price are you willing to pay to see breakthrough in your life?

You're sweating by now. Filling large water jars isn't easy. Your heart is racing. You're on pins and needles, wondering what will happen next. Then Jesus asks you to pour out some of the water and take it to the master of the feast. You have no idea what to think. You're about to either look like the biggest fool in Cana or be part of something big.

If you're being honest, nothing this exciting has ever happened in Cana, the sleepy town you call home. In that moment, you remember a conversation about Jesus you overheard your grandparents having thirty years earlier.

It was something about Mary's pregnancy being unusual. You remember a rumor about her getting pregnant before the wedding, and your grandmother suggesting that Mary's bizarre story might somehow be true ... that the baby was divine. It all comes back to you now. Your grandfather laughed it all off, but you recall your grandmother's quiet response. "He's the Messiah," she said. "Just wait and see."

Suddenly, you feel it—the awe of the moment. And you ask yourself, *What if ...? What if Jesus is the Christ?*

What would you be willing to do if you truly believed that Jesus was the Messiah?

Before you have time to think it through, you grab a cup and dip it into the jar, then you rush toward the master of the feast. And you realize something else ...

You believe.

Read the passage again.

Pause for ten seconds.

The next few moments happen in slow motion. The master of the feast leans forward and takes a sip from the cup. You forget to breathe. What if all you did was for nothing? What if your rising faith in this Messiah was only a figment of your imagination?

But the master of the feast's eyes widen and his smile grows. He wonders aloud why such excellent wine had been hidden. The wine is passed around the dance floor, and soon laughter fills the air. There is joy in this place again.

You look up and notice Mary standing in the background. You swear you can see the shadow of a smile on her face. She knows it too—that Jesus is the true master of this feast!

Spiritual Exercise Week 4

No More Confusion

Matthew 26:20–29

When it was evening, he reclined at table with the twelve. And as they were eating, he said, "Truly, I say to you, one of you will betray me." And they were very sorrowful and began to say to him one after another, "Is it I, Lord?" He answered, "He who has dipped his hand in the dish with me will betray me. The Son of Man goes as it is written of him, but woe to that man by whom the Son of Man is betrayed! It would have been better for that man if he had not been born." Judas, who would betray him, answered, "Is it I, Rabbi?" He said to him, "You have said so."

Now as they were eating, Jesus took bread, and after blessing it broke it and gave it to the disciples, and said, "Take, eat; this is my body." And he took a cup, and when he had given thanks he gave it to them, saying, "Drink of it, all of you, for this is my blood of the covenant, which is poured out for many for the forgiveness of sins. I tell you I will not drink again of this fruit of the vine until that day when I drink it new with you in my Father's kingdom."

Read the passage out loud once.

Now close your eyes and take a few deep breaths. Pray with me: "O God, I pray that You will help me to hear You speak during this time of meditation on Your Word. I open my hands to You. I open my ears to You.

Pause for ten seconds.

Imagine you're one of Jesus' disciples. Earlier that week, you heard and saw Jesus say and do some peculiar things. First, there was the overturning of the tables at the Temple and Jesus warning the religious leaders that they could destroy His body but that He would rebuild it in three days. The religious leaders were furious. For a moment you were scared for Jesus, but you also had no idea what He was talking about.

Jesus got away from the crowd, but the rest of the week seemed heavy. Gone were the days when Jesus showed off with miracles and crazy stuff, like that day when Peter walked on the water or that one evening when Jesus fed the thousands with a loaf of bread! This week felt heavier, which is why Jesus' latest words around the table feel different. It's like Jesus is trying to communicate a message to you. What message is Jesus trying to relay? Why is there such a spirit of heaviness?

And what was that bit with Judas? What does Jesus want him to do? Lately, everything Jesus does seems so … hard to understand.

You think about your own life, what it took for you to be there that night. At first, when you left your job and told your family you'd be traveling with Jesus, they thought you'd lost your mind. But these three years with Him have proven that you made the right choice. People saw all the good Jesus was doing. Some were even talking about Jesus overturning the Roman occupation. You're looking smarter and smarter, and maybe it won't be long before people start asking for your advice on life!

So why did Jesus have to ruin it with news of gloom and doom? Still, when Jesus passes the bread around, you can't help but take your piece and eat it.

Read the passage again.

Pause for ten seconds.

Take a deep breath as you listen to the words of Jesus. Look at Him carefully. What do you see? What makes His words so riveting? Can you sense His heart behind His words? What's driving His intensity tonight? You find yourself leaning in. You hang on to every word He's uttering. Everyone around you is equally riveted. You could hear a pin drop.

What part of the message resonates with you? What part of the message confuses you?

You almost miss the moment when Judas gets up and leaves. Something tells you trouble is on the way. But you can also tell that Jesus is at peace with it all, almost welcoming it.

Read the passage again.

Pause for ten seconds.

How do you respond to Jesus' words? Do you feel afraid for Jesus? Are you tempted to speak up and tell Jesus everything is going to be all right? The problem is, you're not sure you believe it. It crosses your mind that Jesus could fix the impending problem if He wanted to. But why doesn't He seem to be in a hurry to do so?

You're tired. You're a little overwhelmed. You wish Jesus wouldn't speak in riddles. What does He mean when He mentions His Father's kingdom?

Pause for ten seconds.

Your mind wanders over the last three years to the many parables Jesus told about His Father's kingdom. You realize now that Jesus spent a lot of time talking about a coming kingdom. You also remember that day when Jesus spoke about His body being the bread that His followers must eat. You look around and notice the preparation for the Passover.

You think back to the meaning of the Passover. You wonder who will be responsible for buying the lamb for the big meal tomorrow. Will Peter find it, or will you need to go hunt for the sacrifice this year?

You take the cup that Jesus is offering you. You look up and notice His eyes inviting you, comforting you. You lift the cup and drink.

It's in that moment that you finally understand.

Tomorrow, there will be no lamb.

Tomorrow, everything will change.

Spiritual Exercise Week 5

Taste of Victory

Revelation 19:6–16

Then I heard what seemed to be the voice of a great multitude, like the roar of many waters and like the sound of mighty peals of thunder, crying out,

"Hallelujah!
For the Lord our God
   the Almighty reigns.
Let us rejoice and exult
   and give him the glory,
for the marriage of the Lamb has come,
   and his Bride has made herself ready;
it was granted her to clothe herself
   with fine linen, bright and pure"—

for the fine linen is the righteous deeds of the saints.

And the angel said to me, "Write this: Blessed are those who are invited to the marriage supper of the Lamb." And he said to me, "These are the true words of God." Then I fell down at his feet to worship him, but he said to me, "You must not do that! I am a fellow servant with you and your brothers who hold to the testimony of Jesus. Worship God." For the testimony of Jesus is the spirit of prophecy.

Then I saw heaven opened, and behold, a white horse! The one sitting on it is called Faithful and True, and in righteousness he judges and makes war. His eyes are like a flame of fire, and on his head are many diadems, and he has a name written that no one knows but himself. He is clothed in a robe dipped in blood, and the name by which he is called is The Word of God. And the armies of heaven, arrayed in fine linen, white and pure, were following him on white horses. From his mouth comes a sharp sword with which to strike down the nations, and he will rule them with a rod of iron. He will tread the winepress of the fury of the wrath of God the Almighty. On his robe and on his thigh he has a name written, King of kings and Lord of lords.

Read the passage out loud once.

Now close your eyes and take a few deep breaths. Pray with me: "O God, I pray that You will help me to hear You speak during this time of meditation on Your Word. I open my hands to You. I open my ears to You."

Pause for ten seconds.

📍 Describe the scene of this encounter. Take a deep breath. What does it sound like in the atmosphere? What does it feel like? What do you see? Have you ever seen anything this magnificent? What are you praying in these moments? What do you expect will happen?

Read the passage again.
Pause for ten seconds.

Picture yourself as part of the crowd witnessing this remarkable event. When you see the white horse, you fall on your knees. Why do you do that? You look up and see hordes of people sitting at a table waiting for their meal. You recognize some faces. You're surprised to see others. But still, after a few moments, your eyes can't help but be drawn back to the man on the horse. Who is the rider? Do you recognize the face of the one on the horse? What fills you with awe?

You try to hear every word around you. It's so loud and beautiful. You've never heard singing like this before. You find yourself singing too. What are the words you're saying? Is there peace in your heart? Are you anxious for this moment to end?

Pause for ten seconds.

You keep watching. You hear the name the man on the horse is being called: the Word of God. You realize that you're familiar with that term. The Word of God. What are some phrases and words that come to your mind about the Word of God? The whole scene feels like something out of a movie, but it also feels so real.

You're handed an invitation—it says you've been invited to the marriage supper of the Lamb.

All of a sudden, it doesn't feel so foreign anymore. You realize that you are supposed to be here, that you belong. You notice the angels around you singing even louder. This time when you look up, you catch them looking at you. What do they see when they look at you?

You notice one of the angels inviting you to a seat at the table. What fills your heart in that moment? Why are there tears on your face?

One of the angels leans in and whispers that you're not just invited to this marriage supper of the Lamb—you're part of the bride!

Pause for ten seconds.

📍 What goes through your mind when it occurs to you that you're a part of the bride in this story?

You never want this moment to end. You look at Jesus. He seems to know you. He looks at you and holds out His hand.

Your life flashes before you—all your mistakes and moments you wish you'd lived differently appear in your mind but then quickly evaporate. You think about all the sacrifices you made that you didn't think anyone was paying attention to. You think about the moments you shared with Jesus alone. You look to Him and find Him smiling. He knows! He wipes the tears off your face. He smiles. It feels too good to be true.

◉ What do you feel in that moment? What goes through your mind and heart? How does your lifetime with Jesus make you feel in those moments right before the marriage supper of the Lamb? Do you wish you'd sacrificed more? Do you wish you'd trusted Him more? Is there anything you'd do differently if you could just go back one more time?

◉ If you could express your heart to Jesus, what would you say?

Self-Reflection Tool

Answer these questions as you consider how your life is this week.

Heart

1. How is your relationship with God right now?
2. Have you read the Bible this week?
3. What has God been saying to you through your Bible reading?
4. What are you praying for this week for yourself?
5. What are you praying for this week for others?
6. What are you most worried about this week?
7. Is there anything in your life with God that is confusing?

Mind

1. What are you reading this week?
2. What have you done to rest and play this week?
3. Where is Satan attacking you this week, and making you feel like you're not a real Christian?
4. Where are you facing sexual temptation?
5. How are you doing financially? Are you giving sacrificially? Is your spending under control?
6. What are you most thankful for right now?

Relationships

1. How are your relationships going? Which one is not great right now?

2. If I were to ask your closest family and friends how you're doing, what would they say?

3. Is there someone you are having a hard time forgiving?

4. Are you spending time with other Christians? What kinds of activities are you doing together?

5. Who are you most thankful for right now?

Fill-in-the-Blank Answers

Answers to blanks in the lesson main points provided in the session videos.

Session 1: Introduction—Why a Table in the Wilderness?

1. filled
2. provision
3. abundant goodness
4. fellowship (and) communion

Session 2: The Table of Salvation—When I Need to Be Rescued

1. freedom
2. covenant
3. atonement
4. transforms us

Session 3: The Table of Unexpected Belonging—When I Deserve to Be Punished

1. by name
2. loves me unconditionally
3. goodness
4. one of His own

Session 4: The Table of Overflowing Satisfaction—When All I Have Is Empty

1. empty spaces
2. asks of us
3. trust God
4. who Jesus is

Session 5: The Table of Remembrance—When I'm Apt to Forget

1. remember
2. resurrection
3. I am never alone
4. is eventually coming

Session 6: The Table of Eternal Celebration—When Life Is Hard

1. come to pass
2. joy
3. union
4. destroyed
5. satisfied

Notes

1. *Merriam-Webster's Online Dictionary*, s.v. "goodness," accessed May 2, 2023, www.merriam-webster.com/dictionary/goodness.

2. M. G. Easton, "Goodness of God," *Illustrated Bible Dictionary*, 3rd ed. (Thomas Nelson, 1897), www.ccel.org/e/easton/ebd/ebd/T0001500.html#T0001528.

3. N. T. Wright, "The Cross and the Caricatures," *Fulcrum* (April 2007): 1.

4. Easton, "Goodness of God," *Illustrated Bible Dictionary*, www.ccel.org/e/easton/ebd/ebd/T0001500.html#T0001528.

5. Allen C. Myers, ed., *The Eerdmans Bible Dictionary* (Grand Rapids, MI: Eerdmans, 1987), 431.

6. Douglas K. Stuart, *The New American Commentary*, vol. 2 (Nashville, TN: Broadman & Holman, 2006), 272–78; and T. Desmond Alexander, *Exodus* (Downers Grove, IL: InterVarsity Press, 2017), 222–25.

7. Margaret Feinberg, *Taste and See: Discovering God among Butchers, Bakers, and Fresh Food Makers* (Grand Rapids, MI: Zondervan, 2019), 153.

8. David M. Howard Jr., *An Introduction to the Old Testament Historical Books* (Chicago: Moody Press, 1993), 147.

9. Jonathan Edwards, "Types of the Messiah," in *Typological Writings*, ed. Mason I. Lowance Jr. (New Haven, CT: Yale University Press, 1993), 259.

10. Diana V. Edelman, "Lo Debar," in *The Anchor Bible Dictionary*, vol. 4, ed. David N. Freedman (New York: Doubleday, 1992), 345.

11. Got Questions, "What Is the Significance of Lo-debar in the Bible?," accessed June 26, 2023, www.gotquestions.org/Lo-Debar-in-the-Bible.html.

12. C. S. Lewis, *The Weight of Glory* (New York: Macmillan, 1949), 2.

13. Ephesians 2:1–5, you are alive; 1 Corinthians 1:2–3, you are a saint; Ephesians 2:10, you are God's workmanship; Romans 5:17, you are righteous; Ephesians 1:6, you are accepted by God.

14. Timothy Keller, "Lord of the Wine" sermon, November 17, 1996, Redeemer Presbyterian Church, New York, https://gospelinlife.com/downloads/lord-of-the-wine-6467/.

15. Leon Morris, *The Gospel According to John* (Grand Rapids, MI: Eerdmans, 1971), 178.

16. Morris, *Gospel According to John*, 178; and Got Questions, "What Is the Meaning of the Parable of the Wedding Feast?," accessed June 26, 2023, www.gotquestions.org/parable-wedding-feast.html.

17. D. A. Carson, *The Gospel According to John* (Grand Rapids, MI: Eerdmans, 1991), 169.

18. Carson, *Gospel According to John*, 173; and Morris, *Gospel According to John*, 182.

19. Barry J. Beitzel, *The New Moody Atlas of the Bible* (Chicago: Moody, 2009), 243.

20. John MacArthur, *The MacArthur Bible Commentary* (Nashville, TN: Thomas Nelson, 2005), 1589.

21. Megan K. Taylor, "The World's Not a Stage," WordPress, December 16, 2014, https://megankmcnally.wordpress.com/2014/12/16/the-worlds-not-a-stage/.

22. C. S. Lewis, *Mere Christianity* (Westwood, NJ: Barbour, 1952), 115.

23. MacArthur, *MacArthur Bible Commentary*, 2031.

24. MacArthur, *MacArthur Bible Commentary*, 2031.

25. John Piper, "Why Does God Allow Satan to Live?," Desiring God, August 15, 2014, www.desiringgod.org/interviews/why-does-god-allow-satan-to-live--2.

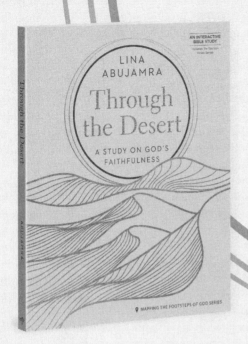

DO YOU LONG TO SEE REVIVAL IN YOUR CHURCH?

ARE YOU DESPERATE FOR A FRESH MOVE OF GOD IN YOUR LIFE?

ARE YOU LOOKING FOR HOPE IN A BROKEN WORLD?

INVITE LINA TO SPEAK AT YOUR EVENT

Lina's mission is to ignite hope in the people of God through the clear and unapologetic teaching of God's Word.

Lina fell in love with teaching the Bible when she was the women's ministry director at a megachurch. Now a popular Bible teacher and podcaster, she speaks extensively at conferences, retreats, and colleges around the world. Her desire is to inspire passion for Jesus in the hearts of God's people and help them experience the beauty of His healing power so they can live in the fullness of who He is calling them to be.

Familiar with pain and brokenness, Lina has authenticity, relatable storytelling, and solid biblical teaching that connects with audiences of all ages and backgrounds.

INVITE LINA:
livingwithpower.org/speaking

LIVING WITH POWER

WE EQUIP CHRISTIANS
TO LIVE WITH POWER BY...

Unapologetically teaching God's Word, providing discipleship resources,
and giving medical and humanitarian aid in disaster areas.

LIVINGWITHPOWER.ORG

estherpress

Our journey invites us deeper into God's Word, where wisdom waits to renew our minds and where the Holy Spirit meets us in discernment that empowers bold action for such a time as this.

If we have the courage to say yes to our calling and no to everything else, will the world be ready?

JOIN US IN COURAGEOUS LIVING

Your Esther Press purchase helps to equip, encourage, and disciple women around the globe with practical assistance and spiritual mentoring to help them become strong leaders and faithful followers of Jesus.

An imprint of

DAVID C COOK

transforming lives together